IMAGES
of America

CHICAGO
ENTERTAINMENT
BETWEEN THE WARS
1919–1939

IMAGES
of America

CHICAGO
ENTERTAINMENT
BETWEEN THE WARS
1919–1939

Jim and Wynette Edwards

ARCADIA

Copyright © 2003 by Jim and Wynette Edwards.
ISBN 0-7385-2330-5

Published by Arcadia Publishing,
an imprint of Tempus Publishing, Inc.
3047 N. Lincoln Ave., Suite 410
Chicago, IL 60657

Printed in Great Britain.

Library of Congress Catalog Card Number: 2003102284

For all general information contact Arcadia Publishing at:
Telephone 843-853-2070
Fax 843-853-0044
E-Mail sales@arcadiapublishing.com

For customer service and orders:
Toll-Free 1-888-313-2665

Visit us on the internet at http://www.arcadiapublishing.com

CONTENTS

The "Westerners" joined the WLS radio staff in the mid 1930s. They specialized in the "sweet and the rollicking songs of the West, but at any time you may expect them to break forth in modern music." Pictured from left to right are Milt Mabie on bass, Larry Wellington on accordion, Dott Massey on violin and trumpet, Louise Massey Mabie on piano and vocals, and Allen Massey on guitar and banjo. Louise, Dott, and Allen were sisters and brother.

The Masseys, reared on a ranch near Roswell, New Mexico, took to singing rather than "cow-punching." Their father was an old-time fiddler who appeared in Chautauquas.

ACKNOWLEDGMENTS

We are indebted to all of those who have previously written about entertainment in Chicago during the 1920s and 1930s, and to those companies such as WGN, WLS, and WBBM, who wrote company histories. We also wish to thank Len Duszlak for the loan of items for this book from his vast collection of Chicago ephemera. Jim Shaffer, a member of CATOE (Chicago Area Theatre Organ Enthusiasts), tracked down pictures of theater organs that are included in the book.

The Chicago Historical Society, the Theater Historical Society of America (especially Grant Meyers), and the Chicago Public Library all provided resources for our education; and the reference librarians at Aurora Public Library have been most helpful and patient with our queries. We thank them all and wish we had another hundred pages available for the book!

INTRODUCTION

Between the two great wars of the 20th century, Chicago was rapidly discarding or radically changing its entertainment pastimes. The great amusement parks such as Riverview and public parks all over the city were still drawing millions of visitors each year, but the new technological inventions and different types of music that came to the forefront during this twenty-year period changed the way that the city's residents amused themselves.

A new type of popular music enjoyed by the emerging lower classes of Chicagoans began to evolve. The waltz was on its way out; ragtime was reaching the end of its tether. Jazz, blues, and swing ruled in the city's thousands of small, ethnic nightclubs, hotels, and dance halls. Chicago's sheet music publishers, radio stations, automatic mechanical music machine manufacturers, record and piano roll makers, and new movie palaces all worked together to keep the city's masses singing and dancing the night away, making Chicago one of the most musical cities in the world. In the world of classical music during the 1920s and 30s, Chicago's various opera companies and symphonies, although struggling with red ink themselves, made traditional classical music available to the masses through a series of free concerts.

Beginning in the 1920s, new mega-movie palaces, like dance halls, were built on the North and South Sides. When the talkies arrived in Chicago, even more elaborate spaces were constructed as theatres than had been built for silent films. Playhouses dotted the city's streets, the ball parks and coliseums were packed, and there seemed to be a speakeasy on every block filling the night air with the sweet sounds of exciting "Chicago Style" music.

After the economy bottomed out in the early 1930s, the entertainment picture changed. Some in the entertainment business found that their jobs were even more secure than in the Roaring Twenties. Big bands and swing music were never bigger, and Hollywood entered its golden age of power. Radio was up and running, quickly becoming the most popular, cheapest form of entertainment, but other forms of entertainment suffered.

By now the phonograph had all but eclipsed player pianos, and Chicago's vaudeville houses were being converted into movie houses. Serious drama took a tumble as did classical music. Chicago confirmed in the 1930s that it continued to have a country connection to the old stockyard days through its love of cowboys and country music shown in its radio programming and reoccurring rodeos staged in the city's great public spaces.

This book is about some of the famous people and events in Chicago during these two decades, but more about the performers who were a smaller part of the entertainment fabric of the city such as those band leaders in ball rooms now mostly forgotten. We designed this book to fascinate, as well as educate. In these all-too-few pages we have collected interesting samples of entertainment in Chicago during the period between World War I and II.

One
END OF AN ERA

It is important for any book attempting to present samples of entertainment for a period to also include, as an introduction, a quick look at the era that came before it for proper perspective. The period of time between the rebuilding of the burned-out city to World War I was vastly different from the Roaring Twenties and the Depression days of the next 20 years. Yet one can sense elements of evolution rather than revolution.

The flappers of the 1920s probably never gave their mothers and grandmothers credit for their quiet work in achieving new freedoms for women. They pressured for their own universities, attended medical schools, worked hard to achieve the right to vote, and became active and vital participants in the arts of Chicago. Women became early serial heroes in the movies and even made the term "cowgirl" a respectable occupation when Annie Oakley, crack sharpshooter, entered a previously male-only occupation.

Women were one of the major driving forces in Chicago during the decades prior to 1920. Chicago's working women tended to be young and single, engaged in such jobs as manufacturing corsets or textiles, book binding, canning, and even meat packing.

The other change to take note of during this time was how new immigrants were transforming the city, and the emergence of Chicago as not only a manufacturing center but also as a think tank of talented young writers, musicians, painters, and journalists.

Carnivals were an early form of entertainment in Chicago that were directed towards all citizens. This is a 1914 carnival that paraded down State Street with the participants all decked out in costumes. Note the use of horses and carriages with trolley tracks down the middle of the street.

VIEW ON WEST MADISON ST.
LOOKING EAST
FROM ALBANY AVE.
1ST JANUARY 1895.

VIEW ON WEST MADISON ST.
1ST JANUARY 1884

Prior to 1884, land around Campbell Avenue and Thomas Street had been farm land. Newly developed lots were offered for sale at $350 each, and by the turn of the century a church, commercial buildings, and rows of houses were on this site. The land value had risen to $1,500. By this time dozens of communities like this one were on the fringe of the city.

The new, middle-class families of Chicago built brick or stone two-story flats with raised basements in neo-gothic style with castle-like turrets. They were often built as attached houses to conserve space. At one time, a structure such as the one shown here could be built for less than $5,000 in the city.

German immigrants formed a strong, core population for the cities of Chicago and Milwaukee. They, like other ethnic groups, opened neighborhood retail shops and breweries and worked in the rail yards and in other semi-skilled and skilled occupations. They also brought their native culture which included a love for German opera. For years, the various opera companies in Chicago capitalized on this by presenting Wagner's operas.

Before there were movie palaces in Chicago, there were large department stores such as Marshall Field's that looked like palaces. Iron skeletal building techniques made it possible to enlarge windows on the first floor to display merchandise. Marshall Field's State Street aisle featured a 357-foot long columned walkway which went from Randolph to Washington Streets.

A favorite restaurant in 1894 was Philip Henrici's Fancy Bakery, Cafe and Restaurant located at 108-110 Randolph Street opposite the Schiller Theatre. Henrici's opened in Chicago 26 years after the Great Fire. The restaurant was 40 by 165 feet and could accommodate 500 customers. During a typical day, they served 2,000 patrons. This photo shows their cake counters on the right.

Uncle Sam, a creation of a cartoonist used to support American expansionism in the 1890s, was used in patriotic parades especially on the Fourth of July. This *c.* 1918 photograph of a flat-bed truck shows Uncle Sam, not in the driver's seat, but riding next to the driver.

Chicago was one of the early centers for aviation. Around the time of the famous Wright Brothers flight in 1903, glider clubs flew their crafts along the lake front. This rare postcard from September 15, 1912, was issued by the first aviation club in Illinois. It is postmarked "Aerial Mail" years before official airmail. The card went aloft that day. Notice famous Chicagoans and Orville Wright in the photograph.

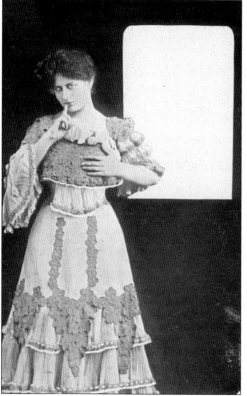

One contribution of Native Americans to the Victorian Era was to turn cigar making in Chicago into a major industry. Pipes were clumsy to load and keep lit, and the cigarette was years away. Tobacco rolled into tubes and called cigars became the smoke of the day. There were hundreds of different types of cigars sold in Chicago under various labels. Cigar makers spiced up their ads by offering a little sexuality with their cigars.

Women's daily dress offered its wearer little comfort in 1910. Underneath countless petticoats and a corset, movement was stilted. Frilled with lacework in a gaudy assortment of strong colors, women went about their everyday life like animated dolls. The placement of the left hand and the finger to the lips makes this a very suggestive postcard for the day.

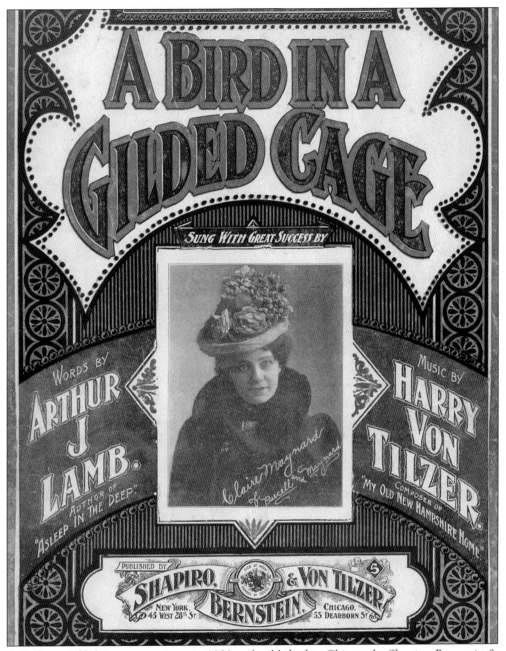

A Bird in a Gilded Cage was written in 1900 and published in Chicago by Shapiro, Bernstein &
Von Tilzer, located at 53 Dearborn Street. It is perhaps one of the most famous songs dealing
with life at the turn of the century, a time when many women were willing to strike out on their
own and not choose the safe route in life.

The song is about a young girl who marries a rich, old man rather than her young lover and
the reference to her life in a cage was a vivid illustration of how restricted some women felt
their lives were or would be if traditions of the older generation were followed. The song was
written by Harry Von Tilzer with lyrics by Arthur J. Lamb. Although originally sung as a ballad,
the song has a bluesy and country feel.

The appearance of women on stage was still controversial in 1900. Howver, acting in amateur productions of musicals such as those written by Gilbert and Sullivan was an acceptable pursuit. Pictured here are women in an amateur production of *The Mikado* given in Chicago around 1900. Many men loved the way women were portrayed in such works—cute, saucy, and mindless.

Women, on the other hand, were not encouraged to poke fun at men with such antics as depicted in this photograph from about the same time. Here "men" enjoy their favorite pastimes of card playing, smoking, and drinking. Everyone in those days played predetermined roles, only men chose the best roles for themselves.

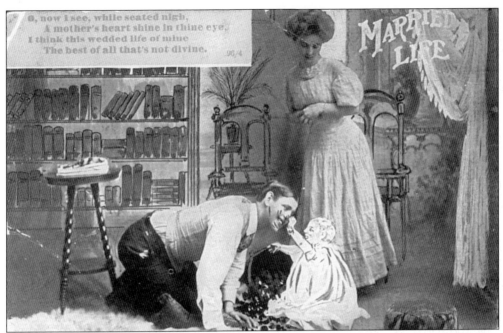

This postcard was mailed from the Stockyards in Chicago by an undertaking business run by Frank Becvar to a Chicago address. The photograph is captioned "Married Life" and shows a father looking pleased as his child smushes berries in his face. Notice that the chairs, bookcase, and baby are drawn on the original photograph! There was no message on this 1896 card.

The first women to become stars in the silent movie days before 1920 were cast in rolls that stressed the innocent, girl-next-door look. Mary Pickford made a fortune hanging onto her pigtails, and countless other young actresses chose the look also. This is a promotional studio photograph of Juanita Hansen as a young innocent.

Young movie-goers in the 1920s, being more worldly than their parents, turned to such heart throbs as Rudolph Valentino and Clara Bow, called the "IT" girl for her box-office sex appeal. Juanita Hansen, just as hundreds of other fame-craving females, changed her look and landed a lead part in the movie *The Secret of the Submarine*.

Patriotism was high around 1900 as the United States was becoming an expansionist power. The Spanish American War was but one example of a continuing road that the United States was traveling on its way to becoming a world power. Even nursery age children were taught passion for flag and country and played "war" with wooden or lead soldiers.

Children's books of the day stressed romantic themes and the world of make believe. Angels and woodland fairies found their way into many popular children's books and play activities. Parents took their children to see Charles Froman's production of *Peter Pan* starring the famous Maude Adams at the Illinois Theatre in 1913.

"Spare the rod, spoil the child" was the watchword associated with teaching. Beating was commonplace in this time. Some men beat their animals, wives, and children. Even in the treatment of the mentally ill, beating and electric shock therapy were used on a daily basis.

From 1870 until the turn of the century, policemen in Chicago tended to be of Irish decent. In many cities the police were recruited from the ranks of the most recent immigrants who worked hard to attain political power and control of the patronage system. The Republican big city press tended to portray the Irish as drunken louts, and pointed to the killing among the Irish when Catholic and Protestant Irish parades were held.

Courtship was under the careful supervision of a member of the girl's family around 1900. The front parlor of the home was where the two love birds got to know each other (no touching allowed). Even when a young couple was lucky enough to visit parks, they still could not escape a chaperone! With the popularity of cars in the 1920s, the car's back seat replaced the parlor couch, chaperones were a thing of the past, and "petting" was mandatory for all flappers!

Many of the old, established modes of transportation such as steamboats, horses with carriage or trolleys, and animal-drawn wagons were to become extinct by World War I, replaced by electric interurban railroad systems and electric, steam, and gasoline run cars and trucks.

The role of the male, as a bridegroom elect, was mentioned in several etiquette books of the day, including the 1905 Collier's *Cyclopedia*. "His first care is to look after a house suitable for his future home, and then, assisted by taste of his chosen helpmates to take steps to furnish it...do well to burn most of his bachelor letters, and to part with, it may be, some few of his bachelor connections...and after the honeymoon...take the reins."

In 1914, record companies took advantage of a country-wide mania to dance the tango, one-step, waltz, and turkey trot. One record producer was the Brunswick-Balke-Collender Company of Chicago, which had made a fortune making billiard tables and bowling alley equipment. Their records were simply called Brunswick.

Dr. Florence Ziegfield established a music school on Michigan Avenue, and when the World's Columbian Exposition came to town, his son Flo turned the "Battery D" building on Michigan Avenue into a dance hall called the Trocadero. Flo's famous Ziegfield Follies almost wound up first in Chicago instead of New York.

Wages in Chicago for the working class seemed low by today's standards, even after the unions got the trades organized in the first decade of new century. Yet one must take into account the general price index for that time. In 1904, if you craved a steak dinner, it was yours for ten cents. Bob's Quick Lunch was located near Clark and Van Buren Streets in 1904.

The upper classes led a gay life in the 1910s. They could attend the Colonial Theatre, billed as having one of the most spacious foyers, in their new $1,050 Marathon Coupe bought from the Marathon showroom at 1712 Michigan Avenue and then dine after the show at Joy Yen Lo's elegant, two-story restaurant at 18-20 North Clark Street.

Blacks were migrating North in significant numbers and creating a whole new neighborhood on Chicago's South Side. This area served, as it had for the Swedish, Irish, German, and Italians, to create a rich, cultural mini-city. Soon the South Side became one of the hottest entertainment areas of the city with rich sounds of jazz clubs that created a Black Chicago Renaissance to rival New York's Harlem Renaissance of the 1920s.

Even during the days of slavery, blacks celebrated life with spirited song and dance brought from Africa. Song and dance were very much a part of their worship services. Theirs was music to dance to; it had a natural beat to it, similar to the human heartbeat.

Black revival meetings usually mixed the secular with the profane with the use of rhythmic spiritual songs. These spirituals were loaded with hand clapping and get-up-out-of-your-seat-and-dance passages. The songs were the roots of what would later be called the blues and jazz.

Minstrel shows, first called "banjo operas," were one of the first uniquely American art forms. After World War I, sometimes instead of featuring black comic side-kicks, German and Jewish side men told dialect stories and jokes, more often than not also lampooning ethnic minorities. Dancing was spirited and featured high-stepping and fancy novelty dancing.

Later in the golden age of movies, black dancers would become world famous. Bill (Bo Jangles) Robinson would tap dance into hearts of theatre goers in the revue movie, *Blackbirds of 1928*. He taught Shirley Temple to dance with him in *The Little Colonel*. The Step Brothers used the latest dance tunes and added flips, splits, and acrobatics to set the dance floor on fire in many movies.

The idea that women were becoming uncontrollable began to sink into the male psyche by 1912 when women threw away their corsets and danced to such songs as *As Long as the Band Will Play*. The new music in Chicago was the bunny hug, the tango, and the turkey trot. President Roosevelt, when he was criticized for his daughter's behavior, said he could either be president or control Alice, he could not do both!

Two

DANCING THE
NIGHT AWAY!

After World War I and through the 1930s, Chicago might well have changed its name to "Musicland," which would have shown the world its importance in the field of nurturing big bands and its people's fascination with dance, hot jazz, and the blues. No matter what kind of music you played or how good a musician you were, there was work for you in Chicago. Prohibition had made having a good time naughty, and people were determined not to let the law keep their spirits down. There were hundreds of nightspots and jazz musicians.

On the North Side, "Bugs" Moran collected his "protection fees," and on the South Side Al Capone took his share. Clarinetist Benny Goodman, guitarist Eddie Condon, and trumpeter Bix Beiderbecke worked in bands that played at mob-controlled gin mills such as the Alcazar, The Three Duces, Paradise, and the Rendezvous. At this time there was great interaction between black and white musicians which helped create a dynamic and new Chicago Style of music. Between 1920 and 1930, 525 black men and 205 women described their occupation as musician. That number was double the reported numbers from the previous decade.

This fusion music would emerge as swing, less hot jazz, and a religious style called the blues, that would sweep the country. Bands got bigger to fill the huge, new dance halls. The bands themselves became vastly different. Some played snooze music for the older crowd, others became swing bands to attract the flaming youth, and boogie woogie arrived to make things even more jivy! Musicians in the Black Belt on Chicago's South Side practically invented the term "Having a Good Time."

Fancy ballrooms, such as the Aragon and those in elegant hotels such as the Drake, had famous bands, but lower down the ladder, orchestras came and went in the city's taxi-dance halls. Men could take a taxi to one of these and, for ten cents a dance, engage a partner and dance the night away. Between 1927 and 1930, there were 36 taxi-dance halls in Chicago similar to the Flamingo.

Chicago had its share of elegant dance hall palaces, decked out with various pseudo-styles from Spanish to Italian to French. The grandest and largest of the lot was the Aragon. The same company built this ballroom that built the French-style Trianon in 1922. The Aragon opened on July 23, 1926, with its magnificent Spanish-Revival architecture. It resembled a Hollywood movie set of a Spanish village square. The patio and sky blue ceiling transported the dancers thousands of miles away to romantic Spain. The Karzas brothers ran their two "Wonder Ballrooms" and spent freely to get the best bands in the land to play for their patrons. Chicago's mayor "Big Bill" Thompson attended the opening of the Aragon. The hall could accommodate 8,000 dancers and was reported to have cost $1,000,000 to construct!

Everything about the Aragon ballroom complex was spacious to accommodate the thousands of dancers. The main floor lobby, grand staircase and promenade all carried out a Spanish theme. The promenade was under the balconies, supported by graceful stone arches that added to the patio effect of the ballroom. Weekly attendance in the 1920s and 30s was around 18,000.

Dancers entered the second level dance floor in the fantasy world of the Aragon by way of a double staircase flanked by two guardian "blackamoors" covered with gold clothing. Three murals faced them as they continued their journey to the right or left as the staircase split. A red carpet and gaudy, multi-colored tiles trimmed the staircase under the coffered ceiling.

Every Tuesday evening from 1926 to 1946, the Aragon held dance classes where beginning dancers were taught how to waltz and fox-trot as well as how to dance the fast-paced one step. The Aragon claimed to have trained more dancers in Chicago than any of the other ballrooms in town. After class there was a "scamper hour" where beginners could dance with 400 experienced regular Aragon dancers.

Another innovation created by William Kartzas for the Aragon was the "singing screen," which was a modern adaptation of the old fashioned sing-a-long. The "mighty organ" played while the lyrics of the song were projected on the screen. The most successful ballrooms and dance halls in Chicago were all located near El stops, and many of the best dance venues had "Gardens" as a part of their names.

The big bands of Harry James, Eddy Duchin, Kay Kyser, Guy Lombardo, Glen Miller, Tommy Dorsey, Sammy Kay, Lawrence Welk, Eddie Howard, Wayne King, and Arti Shaw were booked into either the Aragon or its sister ballroom over the years up to 1947. Kay's motto was, "Swing and Sway with Sammy Kay." Swing and sway may not be quite what the dancers got, but the band was, never the less, very popular over the years.

The Trianon Ballroom, built at Cottage Grove and 62nd Street in 1922, was designed to accommodate 3,000 dancers on the ballroom floor. More people could dance in the promenade areas. The Louis XVI decor was punctuated with red plush curtains and lots of gold on the columns and ceiling. It was thought that such a fancy dance hall would encourage middle and upper class patrons to think that public dance halls were respectable.

Mega star Paul Whiteman and his orchestra were featured in the Trianon's opening week. Whiteman was a flop because no one seemed to realize that the innovative Whiteman's music was made for listening, not dancing! He was paid $25,000 to play the Trianon, an enormous fee for 1924.

Chicago's beautiful people were in attendance at the Trianon's grand opening and were impressed. Pictured here from left to right are Mrs. Potter Palmer, General "Black Jack" Pershing, and Mrs. John Borden. Not pictured, but also in attendance was Mrs. Edward F. Swift. They were invited to a private grand ball on December 5, 1922, one day before the public opening.

Like the Aragon, its sister ballroom on the North Side, the Trianon featured a large lobby and a double grand staircase. The ballroom was dubbed, "The World's Most Beautiful Ballroom." A deep green plush carpet covered the staircase, and the ceiling of the lobby had long, gilded half timbers over a green ceiling.

The Trianon was modeled after the Trianon at Versailles, a small palace given by Louis XVI to his wife Marie Antoinette. The Trianon's first orchestra was created by Del Lampe, and among the musicians was future bandleader Wayne King. This band would play when guest bands were not in residence.

World's Most Beautiful Ballroom

TRIANON

Cottage Grove Ave. at 62nd Street

Has been chosen by the

**Atlantic City
Bathing Beauty
CONTEST
COMMITTEE**

to select

MISS

"CHICAGO"

To represent the City of
Chicago in the

**NATIONAL
Beauty Tournament**

and **BATHING BEAUTY
Pageant**

at Atlantic City

Sept. 2, 3, 4, 5 and 6

Any girl, (white) who has never been
married, between the ages of 16 and
35 can enter the contest for the great
honor of being

"Miss America"

See other side for particulars.

Chicago
Contest
Now On

Closes
August
25th

DAZZLING ELIMINATION REVUES

Now being held in the World's Most Beautiful Ballroom. Come to the Trianon Tuesday, Wednesday or Thursday nights or Sunday Matinee. Bring
your bathing suit which will be your ticket of admission. Enter the contest and win this great honor for Chicago.

It's hard to imagine swing bands playing in this huge ballroom and even more difficult to think what Marie Antoinette would have thought (having lost her head) of the young ladies shedding most of their clothes and participating in "Chicago's Most Beautiful Bathing Girls" contest held in August of 1924. The patrons of this event were promised, "All contestants Appear in Bathing Costume."

Orville Knapp introduced dancers at the Trianon to a whole new style of dance in the 1930s. He had been a big band leader for only three years, and yet in that short amount of time had developed a distinct style which featured exaggerated vibratos and occasional huge bursts of sound followed by sharp diminuendos. Knapp was killed in July of 1936 in a plane he was piloting.

The Merry Garden Ballroom was billed as "Chicago's Chummiest Ballroom" and was famous for its World's Championship Dance Endurance Marathons. The first marathon began on Friday, April 11, 1930 at 9:30 p.m. and ended August 7 at 10:30 p.m. The contest was broadcast daily over WBBM and WCFL.

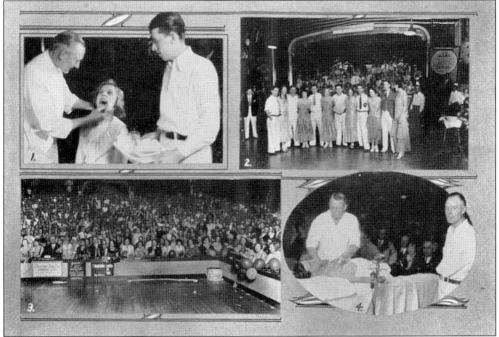

The first marathon drew a packed house. Spectators were cheering for their favorite couple. Shown in the left upper corner is Ann Gerry receiving her daily dental examination. Upper right, Ethel Kendall is presenting gold metals to the eleven dancers commemorating the breaking of the previous world's record of 1,800 hours, 21 and a half minutes. Lower left shows a crowd watching the marathon: lower right, two members of the medical team examining a fatigued dancer.

35

The winners of the first marathon were Ann Gerry and Mike Gouvas, who were first teamed with other partners when the contest began. On hand to make sure no one lacked for medical attention was a medical unit with four foot specialists, a dentist, two nurses, and other assorted personnel. The Merry Garden Orchestra, under the direction of Frank Owen, had a nightly request dance show on radio station WCFL.

The rules of the dance marathon were exacting. Dancers had to dance 57 minutes out of every hour with a three minute rest period. They had to dance, walk, or raise their heels and toes at least six times per minute. The dancers could also choose to dance continuously for five hours then rest 15 minutes. They rested on cots at ring-side.

Opposite: You cannot keep a great big band down for long. Ben Pollack, drums master in 1929, had the dream orchestra with Benny Goodman on clarinet, Jack Teagarden on trombone and legendary Jimmy McPartland on cornet. But the band broke up. By 1936, Pollack was in the grove again with a band that consisted of more undiscovered talent: Harry James and Shorty Sherock on trumpet and pianist Freddy Slack.

His band proved to be a training ground for other great, swinging big bands. For all the great musicians that played in the Pollack band over the years, the band itself was never considered one of the best. After 1938, Ben had a small Dixieland group where he played drums and later on he ran his own club and became a record producer.

Early black jazz clubs were smaller than their white counterparts as a rule, which resulted in creating a unique dance style. Ethyl Waters appeared in New York at a black-only night spot where the size of the dance floor was so restrictive that the only dancing possible was characterized by standing and shuffling feet. This was called "dancing on a dime." At Bert Kelly's Stables, singing waiters and dancing cooks added to the mood.

Hall Kemp and his orchestra began a lengthy engagement in Chicago in 1934 at the famous Blackhawk restaurant. They developed a soft and sensuous sound which sky-rocketed them to national attention. When the band was formed in his college years, it was a jazz band. In later years, it would go back and forth from a sweet sound to swing style.

One of Bert Kelly's Jazz Band's venues was the ballroom. Right before 1920, he was playing for the Booster's Club on the roof of the Morrison Hotel. Although New Orleans was the birthplace of jazz, the modern (1920s) jazz orchestra originated in Chicago and California. It consisted of two saxophones, cornet, trombone, violin, banjo, piano, and drums with two cymbals.

The Empire Room in the Palmer House was one of the prestigious dinner dance rooms in Chicago. One ad stressed that it was "famous for its brilliant revues and name bands presented at dinner and supper nightly." Its elegant bandstand with gold music stands was the epitome of good taste. When the Charleston fizzled, the tango took its place in these elegant surroundings.

Veloz & Yolanda

Dancers Veloz & Yolanda, stars in New York, appeared in the Empire Room. Additional acts booked were the Merriel Abbott's Dancers, twelve girls from Ciro's in London. There was continuous dining, but dancing and entertainment began at 6:30 p.m. Minimum charges after 9 p.m. on Saturdays was $2.50 with featured dinners costing $2.00 in 1933.

Season's Greeting FROM Guy Lombardo AND HIS ROYAL CANADIANS

Put four spoons full of sugar in your coffee and you will have the sweetness level of the music of Guy Lombardo and His Royal Canadians. They began as unknowns from Windsor, Ontario. One of the band's secrets to staying popular was its ability "to embrace all types of music—even Calypso," according to Lombardo. His appearances at the Trianon and Aragon ballrooms in Chicago caused the band's popularity to soar.

Ben Bernie, "The Ol' Maestro," played at College Inn in the Sherman House Hotel. His was one of the bands playing at the Chicago World's Fair in 1934. He had a young singer from Nashville, Dinah Shore, singing commercials for him on his coast-to-coast radio broadcasts, but when she went to work for Eddie Cantor, he took credit for discovering her.

The Pabst Blue Ribbon Casino across the street from the Century of Progress Fair hired four famous dance bands to entertain visitors. The casino featured a revolving platform for all the dance bands so that guests could enjoy continuous music in the outdoor dancing pavilion. The indoor casino could hold 1,000 guests and the open air garden held 2,500.

In the same year that Bert Kelly invented the term jazz band, Isham Jones, saxophonist and pianist, came to Chicago. Jones became an over-night sensation when he organized a band to play at the Old Green Mill, a popular Chicago resort. He soon made his way to the "million dollar dance emporium," the Rainbow Garden, and he also played at the Hotel Sherman's famous College Inn.

Isham Jones and his band toured the country and even played a long engagement in London. He was a noted songwriter as well. One of his tunes was *Spain*, a tango, which was played by the Whiteman band in an arrangement by Ferde Grofe. His biggest hit recording of all was *I'll See you in My Dreams*. He recorded the famous Al Jolson/Vincent Rose hit song *Avalon* with his Rainbow Orchestra for the Chicago record company, Brunswick.

MAIN DINING
(Walnut) ROOM

BISMARCK
HOTEL
CHICAGO

The dance bands that appeared in the Walnut Room of the Hotel Bismark were less renowned than the bands that appeared in the larger ballrooms. During the days of the tango's popularity, the Leonard Keller Orchestra mounted productions that featured a lead singer with a dance troupe of nine to get the diners in the mood for dancing the sultry music.

The Continental Room in the Stevens Hotel was one of the hot spots for those who liked a good orchestra and a novelty piano player in the style of Zez Confrey. Ray Bargy was the pianist and the orchestra was put together by Armin Hand. The decor of the room was Art Deco while the Stevens Grand Ball Room downstairs was Louis XV.

The Chez Paree at 610 Fairbanks Court was Chicago's premiere spot from the 1930s to the 1950s. There was never a more sophisticated and elegant Art Deco dance room constructed in Chicago. Its stage was graced by such classy acts as Lena Horne, Sophie Tucker, and Mae West. They featured a great chorus line called the Chez Paree Adorables.

For the less sophisticated crowd, those who wished to see "adorable" females with a few less clothes as they entertained, Violet Downs was the place. Besides five acts of girls! girls! girls!, you got free spaghetti on Friday nights. Sammy Smith, the manager, wrote on the back of this postcard, "Best show we ever had on these two nights Friday & Saturday." Music was provided by the Sammy Smith Orchestra.

Three
RIDE 'EM, COWBOYS

Hard as it is to imagine, at one time Chicago was every bit a "Cowtown" as Abilene or Denver were. When Chicago began growing from a village to a town, and when railroads began to use the settlement as a central hub for transportation, livestock came into the city and Chicago was chosen as the point at which the buying and selling of beef headed for the eastern markets took place. The many men who took care of the livestock in the yards south of town were as much deserving of the name "cowboys" as their more western, branding, and trail-driving counterparts.

The World's Fair of 1893 confirmed the Chicago's cowboy connection when Buffalo Bill Cody brought his Wild West show to the Exposition and presented the first rodeo ever held.

Cowboys had just about disappeared from the trail by the time movie studios made their home in Chicago in the early 1900s. Essanay Movie Company, sensing a public clamor for movies with cowboy heroes, cranked out hundreds of short westerns which made their way into movie theaters. Essanay created the character of Broncho Billy who made a western every week for 375 weeks in and around Chicago. The studios were located in the 1300 block of West Argyle Street.

When radio stations were established in Chicago, they found a ready market for cowboy lore singing and bronc (a shortened name for Mexican word broncho, meaning "mean") riding over the air. Rodeos became part of the entertainment scene between the wars.

The cowboy is a powerful, romantic figure. Much about the cowboy has been exaggerated for public consumption. Life on the trail was brutal for man and beast. Frank Harris wrote My Reminiscences as a Cowboy, where he traced his journey on a cattle drive headed for Chicago. He arrived at the same time as the Great Fire of 1871. Harris wrote that the real cowboys were not usually Christianized characters and that they hated their horses and most of all, cows.

Adventure stories featuring gun-shootin' hard riding cowboys appeared toward the end of the 19th century. Newspaper print, serialized versions of cowboy adventures, and novels created western cowboy heroes by the dozens. Toward the end of the Victorian age down through most of the 20th century, cowboy heroes ruled in literature, movies, and television.

SAY WHEN READY AND I'LL SHOOT.

Real cowboys did not fit the public's image of frontier heroes. Few were handsome, few were gunslingers or even carried a gun, and few had pretty girlfriends due to their on-the-trail aroma. Many early movie cowboys were also short, being only slightly over five feet in height. In addition, real cowboys could rarely sing on key or play a musical instrument with finesse.

It was the invention of the refrigerated railroad car in the 1870s that made Chicago the butchering and processing capital of the world by the 1880s. Philip Armour said he lost $10.21 on each head of cattle on the consumable beef but made a profit of $10.80 on the cows "unwanted remains." From this part of the animal came margarine, brushes, combs, bouillon, musical instrument strings, glue buttons, chess pieces, and neat's foot oil.

Here is a birds-eye view of Chicago's Union Stockyards taken about 1912. At that time, the yards covered an area of 400 acres and had 3,300 pens. Within the yards were 20 miles of streets and 87 miles of railroad track. At the time of World War I, the stock yards were slaughtering and processing 15 million animals per year, thus earning the city more nick-names—Porkopolis and Beefopolis.

The meat packing buildings were located near the stockyards. One meat packer, Armour & Company, had 70 acres of work flooring and employed about 5,000 men. If you counted all workers in all packing houses in Chicago during the busy season, the number could be as high as 25,000 workers.

TO
Mr. J. H. Brinkerhoff

CHOICE CUT
OF
PRIZE BEEF

INTERNATIONAL
Live Stock
EXPOSITION
UNION STOCK YARDS
CHICAGO
U. S. A.
1936

In the 1920s, the stockyards operated much as they had in the beginning. They were an open, free, and public market. Any owner of livestock could send his livestock in and sell it himself or employ anyone he chose to sell for him. The management of the yards did not buy, sell, or kill the livestock. By 1948 over a billion animals had been sold in the Chicago Stockyards.

CHICAGO UNION STOCK YARD'S SIX HORSE TEAM

1416-29

In 1929, this team of six Clydesdale geldings, each weighing about a ton, won top awards at the International Live Stock Exposition in Chicago and at shows in other cities. The team was owned by the Union Stock Yard & Transit Company. At this time, an average of two million dollars worth of livestock passed through Chicago yearly, earning Chicago the title of "The Great Central Market."

At the first International Grand Champion Steer Sale in 1900, the winner was a 1,430-pound Angus which had been fed by Stanley Pierce from Creston, Illinois. It sold for $1.50 per pound. The record price for International purple ribbon winners was $10.71 in 1948 for a 1,200-pound Aberdeen-Angus steer raised by C.E. Yoder & Son.

A 1925 Chicago rodeo book billed the not-yet-completed Chicago municipal Stadium (later Soldiers' Field) as "Cowboy Land on the Lake Front." It noted that the Stadium, when completed, "will have cost $5,000,000 and will have a spectator capacity of nearly 100,000...making it the largest municipal arena in the world."

This great indoor space for events replaced an earlier structure. Simply called the Chicago Stadium, it was built in 1929 at 1800 West Madison. Democratic conventions were held here as well as rodeos. It had what was billed as the world's largest pipe organ to keep the crowds stirred up with enthusiasm. Now demolished, towards the end of its life it was used mainly for hockey and basketball games.

Before a sparse crowd at the Century of Progress Rodeo in Soldiers' Field, a bulldogger grabs for a horn and the jowl of the racing steer. "Bulldogging" is the old name for steer wrestling where the cowboy attempts to throw a steer by his horns. Hidden from sight is another mounted rider who is the cowboy's assistant.

A hazer and bulldogger catch one in the starting line. The hazer is the bulldogger's helper who, after the bulldogger leaps from his pony to the steer, takes away the pony. The hazer also prevents the bulldogger from being gored when he finally leaves the steer. This picture was also taken at the lakefront stadium at the Century of Progress rodeo.

The cowboys' bronc-riding contest was one of the most dangerous and exciting events at a rodeo. Riders could be disqualified for any number of fouls such as loosing a stirrup, changing hands on the rein or losing rein, being bucked off, wrapping reigns around the hand, or hitting the horse with a hat or hand. This photo shows a bronc rider reaching for a "sky hold."

The trick and fancy-roping contest was only entered by cowboys skilled in lariat manipulation. Will Rogers, the movie, vaudeville star, and humorist, was a world class fancy-roping cowboy. He called all his lariat tricks "little tricks...because there are not any really big rope tricks" when he cracked jokes in theaters. Here is a champion lariat cowboy practicing a two-rope trick before performing at the Century of Progress rodeo.

Out of the 13 events which were part of Tex Austin's 1927 rodeo held in Chicago, only two featured women; the Cowgirls' Bronc Riding and the Cowgirls' Trick and Fancy Riding contests. In 1926, the cowgirl and cowboy Trick and Fancy Riding contest were held separately, but in 1927 they competed together. Mable Strickland, shown here, was one of four female riders in the event.

Rodeos were held often during the 1930s and 40s in Chicago stadiums. The Chicago Stadium Corporation hosted the 1941 World's Championship Rodeo Contest from October 17 to November 2. The announcer for the contest was NBC's Jack Story, famous for his coverage of the National Air Races and state fair dirt track racing.

In the 1930s, the Drake Hotel in Chicago knew that city slickers wished to play cowboy and offered a Western dude ranch experience for their guests. John H. Stevens had an office in the hotel and represented Rising Sun Ranches for Guests, located in the Rockies at Bozeman, Montana. The advertisements claimed that "Here is Freedom and the Peace of Ancient Mountains."

This photograph was found in a scrapbook of a person who collected Chicago memorabilia and was bought by the authors. It is assumed that the two gussied-up singers were from Chicago. It is signed, "To Mr. Klein With Best Wishes Tucson Ted and Yodeling Bobbie" and appears on a postcard, c. 1920.

Roy Rogers brought his World's Championship Rodeo to Chicago where he and his wife, Dale Evans, performed in the arena along with Jim Eskew Jr., who presented an "Exhibition of Cotton Rope Spinning." Roy's famous performing horse, Trigger, performed as well as long-time associates Bob Nolan and the Sons of the Pioneers. Roy Rogers said once that he liked to spend time "the way we like best, that is around horses and cowboys." He had strong feelings about the heritage of the American Cowboy. "Rodeos are as much the national pastime as baseball, and the cowboy with his ten gallon hat and boots is just as much a part of the national scene as the kid with the ball and bat. And since the fall of each year is World Series time, I am bringing you the Cowboy's World Series."

THE SINGING COWBOY

Roy Rogers and Gene Autry were perhaps the top two singing cowboys in the movies. Autry got his start singing on the WLS Barn Dance in the 1930s, calling himself the "Oklahoma Yodeling Cowboy." His sentimental ballads were popular with the WLS audience. One of his first recordings was *That Silver Haired Daddy of Mine*, but his most famous recording was *Rudolph the Red Nose Reindeer*, recorded years later.

Early television star and comedian George Goebel was once called "Little Georgie." He began his entertainment career singing for the WLS Barn Dance. Born in Chicago in 1919, Goebel was the youngest member of the cast. His act featured a tiny ukulele, but he performed country and cowboy songs as well as the adult performers.

A Chuck Wagon Race was held in the Grant Park Stadium in 1925. Each outfit consisted of a chuck wagon drawn by a four-horse team, driver, helper, and two mounted outriders. They had to detach their horses, set up a pot rack and make a fire under the coffee pot. Five seconds were added to the time if they hit a barrel or lost part of their equipment.

"The Ridge Runners" with their leather boots and hickory shirts made this mountain country music group easy to pick out in a crowd. Pictured from left to right are Slim Miller, John Lair, Karl Davis, Linda Parker, Red Foley, and Hartford Taylor. Red Foley would go on to fame as the man who took jazz and the blues and fused them into a unique country gospel sound.

Truck drivers have always seemed to equate their lifestyle with that of the cowboy. Cowboys "drove" long distances; so did the truck drivers. Truck drivers tend to like country music and believe in values supposedly shared by those who first settled on the prairie. Many of the drivers that stopped at Clara and Roy's "the Truck Drivers' Social Club" at Eighteenth and Wabash probably attended rodeos in Chicago every chance they could when passing through town.

The WLS Barn Dance's next generation of cowboy stars would include Bob Atcher "Top Hand of the Cow-hands'" shortly after World War II. Atcher was no synthetic cowboy, although in this picture he is sure dressed like one. He is shown here with his wife Maggie, their son Robin, a $25,000 palomino, Maggie's horse, Robin's colt, and his famous hand-made silver mounted saddle. Atcher made over 300 Columbia records by 1953.

Four

MECHANICAL
MUSICAL MARVELS

The introduction of a player piano using rolls of punched paper first came to the general public's eye around 1900 when the Aeolian Company introduced their "Pianola" player piano. Designed as a push-up unit to be used in front of the piano, this early machine could play rolls cut with a 65 note range, as well as the soon-to-be-standard 88 note roll. The machines of this time were powered by an operator pumping with his feet to create a vacuum that ran the machine. Before World War I, Aeolian Company and dozens of other companies began to miniaturize the player mechanism and place it within the cabinet of pianos. By the 1920s player pianos had gone high-tech with electrically driven units and elaborate realistic sounding pianos and rolls that could express a full range of dynamics. In 1923, there were almost 200,000 player pianos produced in the United States, and at one point more players were sold than standard pianos! Chicago was home base for many of the great player piano firms such as Melville Clark, Gulbransen, Cable, Brinkerhoff, and roll makers such as Q.R.S., Imprerial, Mel-O-Dee, Universal Capital, and U.S. Rolls.

Chicago excelled in one particular field of player pianos manufactured in the U.S., the production of coin-fed mechanical musical machines that sold to businesses as money makers—a nickel at a time. Today a business might have a juke box or computer game on hand, but back in the 1920s and 30s mechanical music machines provided entertainment. They were used in movie theatres, dance halls, ice cream parlors, pool halls, skating rinks, bordellos, and in countless other businesses. Chicago's Nickel Grabbers ruled!

Although player pianos came with levers in front of the keyboard which provided for adjustment of tempo and dynamics, most people just set the tempo to one spot and pumped away. The player piano was a popular form of home entertainment for the young and old alike. This advertising card was mailed from the John Church Co. at 260 Wabash Avenue to a Mr. Arthur R. Douglas in Wheaton by salesman, Ernest L. Kolbaum.

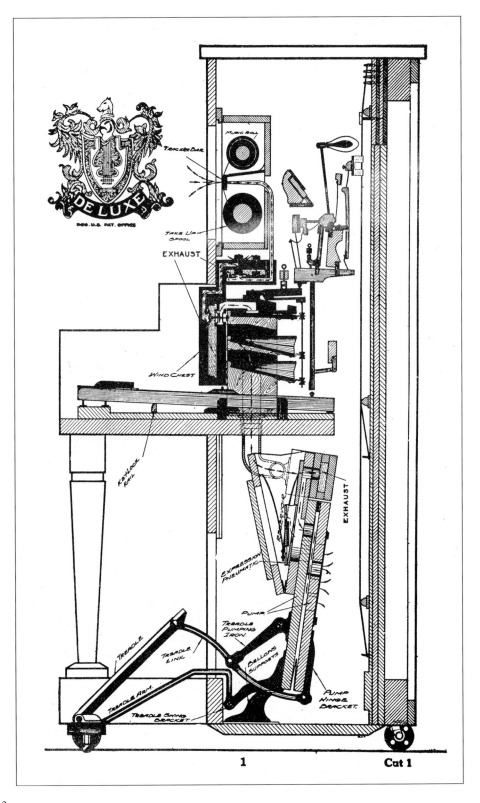

DE LUXE
REG. U.S. PAT. OFFICE

TRACKER BAR

MUSIC ROLL

TAKE UP SPOOL

EXHAUST

WIND CHEST

KEYBED RAIL

EXHAUST

EXPRESSION PNEUMATIC

PUMP

TREADLE PUMPING IRON

TREADLE

TREADLE LINK

TREADLE ARM

BELLOWS SUPPORTS

TREADLE SWING BRACKET

PUMP HINGE BRACKET

1   Cut 1

60

Opposite: At the turn of the 20th century, air pressure power was all the rage. It was supposed to be used to run a New York subway system by creating pressure that would propel the cars through the tunnels. The system proved impractical but the pressure idea was used to transport documents through tubes between banks and in department stores to send cash payments to the office. Change came back through the tube to the sales person and customers. The electrical vacuum cleaner is in many ways like a foot pumped or electrical player piano. This diagram shows a foot-pumper version of a player where the operator pumps back and forth on two pedals which fills large bellows with air. Smaller bellows, called pneumatics, were connected above the keyboard. A roll is placed in a spool box and the moving roll with punched holes travels over a tracker bar with slots in it. As a hole in the roll travels over its mate on a tracker bar, a small bellow is moved and a rod pushes down a piano key.

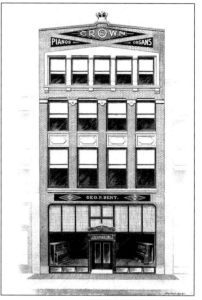

Wabash Avenue was home to the various musical trades for many decades. Lyon and Healey was located nearby, as was Orchestra Hall, the Fine Arts Building, and the Auditorium Theatre. Their presence helped create a musical community. Piano manufacturers and distributors also had showrooms along the avenue. Crown Piano Company maintained its general offices and showrooms at 211-213 Wabash Avenue.

Piano factories were located on the edge of the city, but some piano makers moved their factories to rural cities. Melville Clark, a pioneering player piano innovator moved his factory to DeKalb. Crown Piano Company stayed within the city to build its factory which was located at the corner of Washington and Sangamon Streets. This six-story block-long factory was typical of Chicago's mechanical musical piano factories.

The 1920s were years during which mass advertising grew into a major service industry. Advertising agencies used every trick in the book to sell the products. The typical player piano ad stressed family values. In this classic ad for Gulbransen Company's upright player piano (made in Chicago) the company stressed that the family would remain close and that both children and parents enjoy playing and singing along with the music roll. Popular music rolls had the words to the song printed on the roll so that sheet music was not needed to have a sing-a-long. Gulbransen had other advertisements that said their pianos were easy to pump, even for small children.

Opposite: When Teddy Roosevelt visited the Seattle World Exposition, he was so impressed with an automatic music machine that he dubbed it one of the finest American inventions ever and ranked it up there with the reaper, color photography, and the steam turbine. What he heard was an automatic violin-playing machine called the "Violano-Virtuoso" that was manufactured by the Mills Novelty Company of Chicago. A version of the machine was patented in 1909, and the U.S. Patent Office declared it one of the eight great inventions of that decade. The violin played in conjunction with a 44-note piano action in the base of the cabinet. The notes were played by electric solenoids.

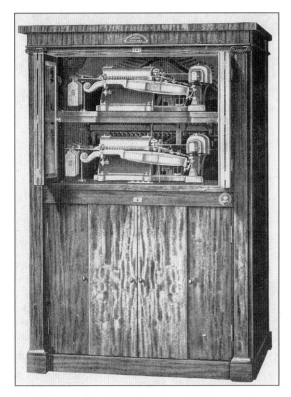

Mills Novelty Company sold this coin-operated machine to drug stores, cigar stores, restaurants, arcades, and a multitude of other small merchants wishing to increase revenue and provide free entertainment for their businesses. Shown here is their two-violin machine that was sold all over the world. The inventor of this marvelous machine was Henry K. Sandall. A small rotating wheel made contact with the violin strings to make sound.

Mills also marketed a "Violano Orchestra" to work in concert with their "Violano-Virtuoso." This machine added bass and snare drum, Chinese tom-tom, wood clapper, and cymbals. The combined effect was that of a four or five piece orchestra, perfect for tea dancing. The most popular model for movie theaters featured one violin above the keyboard and three stacked violins beside the abbreviated keyboard.

The music best suited for the various Mills Violanos was salon music such as *Meditation* from the opera *Thais*. Refined, light, classical music was also a natural for this machine. Other nickel-grabber machines were marketed to saloons and tobacco stores. The perfect locations for Violanos were cafes, up-scale hotel lobbies, candy stores, and elegant family residences.

Operators Piano Company of Chicago manufactured a line of coin-operated pianos and orchestrons that have become the favorites of automatic mechanical music collectors world wide. One of the reasons for the acclaim is that the "O" style music roll, which this machine uses, allows for more music, or simply "more bang for the buck." This company began manufacturing in Chicago in 1904 and operated into the early 1930s.

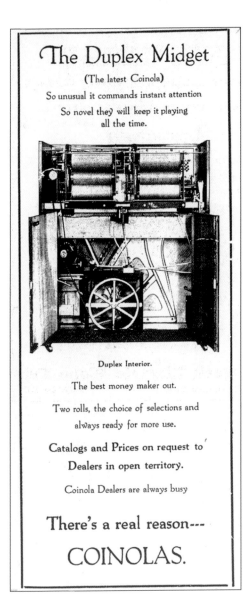
Shown here is the popular Coinola Duplex Midget. It featured two long playing rolls which stopped and started with each nickel deposited. The Midget was a forerunner of the jukebox with multiple record choices. Marketed as the Midget "A," it had five upgrades to become an orchestron. The Midget "X" with its gutsy xylophone was a Chicago favorite. The company, located at 715 North Kedzie Avenue, called their machines "Pianos that Pay."

Western Electric Piano Company moved their Chicago factory from 429 West Superior Street to a new factory at 900-912 Blackhawk Street in 1926. The new factory was twice the size of the older one. B.C. Waters was one of this company's officers of which A.F. Larson was president. This company entered the marketplace late, in 1924, with their "Selectra" orchestrons (machines that claim to sound like a whole orchestra).

The most famous device that Western Electric Piano Company produced was its "Derby" model which was a small electric piano with a small, round racetrack behind glass with miniature riders. When the music stopped, the rider nearest the post was the winner. It was a great unofficial gambling machine!

J.P. Seaburg Piano Company had various locations in Chicago. They were located at 1508 Dayton Street and also on music row at 274 Wabash Avenue. Begun in 1907, by the 1920s Seaburg had a line of nine or more coin-fed, piano-based machines. Some had extras such as drums, cymbals, and xylophones.

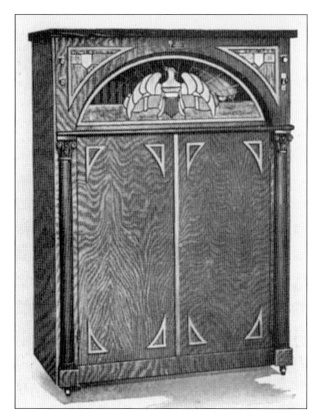

Two of the most collectable of all the Seaburg orchestrons were the model "K," with its magnificent stained glass eagle, mandolin and xylophone attachments, and its larger "KT" with the same features but also featuring castanets and tambourine. Coin-fed mechanical musical instruments were at the zenith of their popularity in 1925. The "KT" was displayed at a music convention in the Drake Hotel that year.

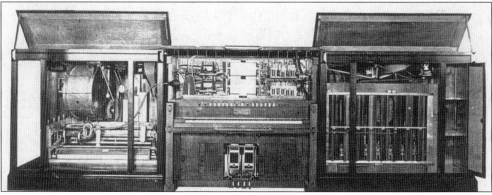

If you wanted a lot of music, the mechanical "orchestras" created for the pits of silent movie houses fit the bill. Seeburg had a magnificent Pipe Organ Orchestra, Style T. Operators' Piano Company featured the "Reproduco" line of theater organs. This "Fotoplayer" was a typical pit machine that had pull cords that produced such sounds as train whistles, fog horns, wind, pistol cracks, and crockery smashes. Who said the silent movies were silent?

Five
THE PLAY'S THE THING

During the 1922-23 theatre season there were 98 shows, of which 22 were musicals, that played in 19 downtown theaters, many of which had been built in 1910. But by 1941 the lights were still burning in only six, despite the efforts of the WPA Federal Theatre Project in the late 1930s. The Great Northern and the Blackstone were the venues for most of the WPA-produced works.

Non-professional, smaller theater productions helped take up the slack for those who wanted to see live theater. Ethnic theatre companies presented works from their homelands. The Yiddish Theater presented several plays of high quality. It was said the work of the Chicago Swedish Theater compared favorably to that in Sweden. *Vermlandingarne*, F.A. Dahlgren's folk play, was a popular piece for this group in Chicago.

Jane Addams, of Hull House fame, believed in the theater's power to shape public opinion. Her Demi-Tasse Players began to present one act plays in 1924 every other Tuesday evening immediately after dinner at Hull House. Laura Dainty Pellham directed the Hull House players until her death in 1924. Schools and churches also produce plays and the audience was always full of family members for these productions.

The theater program cover art was outstanding in the 1920s. Join us as we look at some of the theaters of the 1920s and 1930s in Chicago and the cover art printed for those productions.

Blossom Time was written in 1921 by Dorothy Donnelly. The music, by Franz Schubert and H. Berte was adapted by Sigmund Romberg. The first Chicago performance opened March 12, 1922, and ran for 19 weeks. This perennial favorite was brought back to Chicago eight more times before 1940 for two to eight weeks each time, usually by the Messrs. Schubert. It played at the Apollo, the Auditorium, Studebaker, and the Grand Opera House.

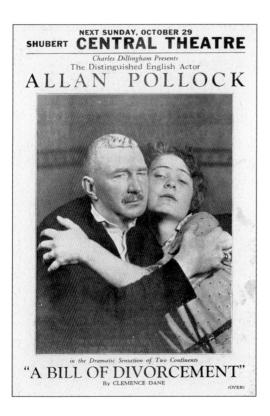

The Central Theatre, built in 1893 with 850 seats, was once known as Steinway Hall. It had four supporting posts that obscured sight lines and the acoustics were said to be poor. Light opera and musical productions were the usual fare at the Central. *Bill of Divorcement* played for two weeks at the Central in 1922.

The Apollo Theatre opened with *The Passing Show of 1921* in May of that year, but there had been eight years of "passing shows" at other theatres before the production moved to the Apollo. This theater has had many names such as Schubert's Apollo, the Olympic, Grand Opera House, Music Hall, Cristy's Opera House, New Chicago, and Kingsbury Hall, and it has been located in more than one address.

The LaSalle Theatre was built in 1910 and was alive with plays until April 1927 when it closed to become a motion picture house. This program is for *Oh, My Dear*, which was brought to the LaSalle in January 1920. It was billed as the sixth annual Princess Theatre musical comedy success. The cast members' names are prefaced with Mr. or Miss., a practice that was discontinued in 1925.

The Cat and The Canary was a mystery melodrama presented at the Princess Theatre that ran from September 2, 1922, through March 11, 1923. A notice on the program page states, "This theatre does not advertise in the *Chicago Evening Post* because of its persistency in printing untruthful statements about the Messrs. Shubert, their theatres and attractions." It sounds as if someone received some bad press here.

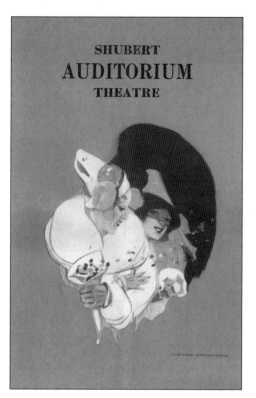

The Clyde W. Riley Advertising Company began publishing Chicago theater programs in 1894. Their beautiful covers were used for many different theatres and for several years. This cover was used in the Sam H. Harris Theatre and LaSalle Theatre in addition to the Auditorium Theatre. In 1929 *Playgoers (The Magazine in the Theatre)* stated that they were the official publication of all Chicago leading theaters playing stage attractions. The Chicago company *Chicago Stagebill* began printing all Chicago theaters' programs in 1938.

Cort Theatre was built in 1910, the same year 25 neighborhood theatres were built. It was demolished in 1934, one of the many causalities of the Great Depression. This program for the 1924 performances of *The Deluge* is unusual for the time in that it gives information on the origination of the play. Henning Berger was a Swedish playwright who wrote about American life from his experiences as an immigrant.

This 1925 program for the Illinois Theatre is for the musical play *Stepping Stones* with Fred and Dorothy Stone. The music for this play was by Jerome Kern. The Illinois, built in 1900, was the first building in Chicago to be constructed solely for theatrical performances. It was razed in 1934.

The Central Theatre used Paul H. Fieberg Co. to print their program for *Welcome Stranger* in 1924. This melodrama ran for twelve weeks that fall. It was presented by Carl A. Barrett, owner of Central Theatre, by special arrangement with Sam H. Harris. The Central had stage presentations until February 1934. After that, it became a motion picture house.

73

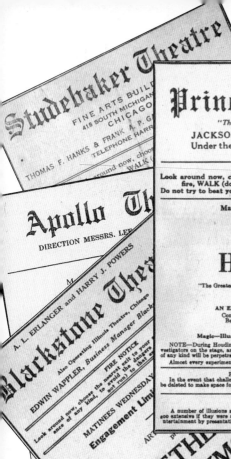

These playbills were printed on half sheets of paper and had no ads in them. They are all from between September 1924 and October 1925. Ethel Barrymore was playing at the Blackstone, reportedly to have the finest theatre architecture west of New York. Houdini was presented at the Princess and that program offered challenges to the public and exposed secrets of various mediums.

Mae West was the hot ticket at the Apollo from January 29, 1929, to April 28, 1929, when she appeared in *Diamond Lil*. The play moved on to the Great Northern in April. The Apollo presented a variety of programming, from minstrel and vaudeville to Shakespeare and Theodore Thomas' orchestra.

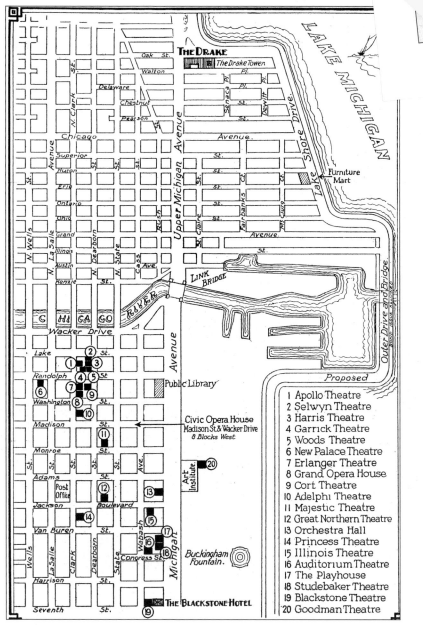

The map shows downtown Chicago with the following theater locations listed:

1 Apollo Theatre
2 Selwyn Theatre
3 Harris Theatre
4 Garrick Theatre
5 Woods Theatre
6 New Palace Theatre
7 Erlanger Theatre
8 Grand Opera House
9 Cort Theatre
10 Adelphi Theatre
11 Majestic Theatre
12 Great Northern Theatre
13 Orchestra Hall
14 Princess Theatre
15 Illinois Theatre
16 Auditorium Theatre
17 The Playhouse
18 Studebaker Theatre
19 Blackstone Theatre
20 Goodman Theatre

There were 98 shows, of which 22 were musicals, produced in 19 theaters in the 1922-23 season. The number of playhouses remained constant from 1922 to 1930, the date of this map, but the players changed. Gone were the Central, Cohan's Grand, Colonial, LaSalle, Olympic, and Powers. In their places were the New Palace, Erlanger, Grand Opera House, Adelphi, Majestic, and Goodman. The Chicago Symphony Orchestra and the opera had moved from the Auditorium to their own, new homes. The Great Depression was hard on performers, but especially on the theaters. The Playhouse and Adelphi closed and became motion picture houses in 1921, The Garrick in 1933, and Apollo and Illinois in 1934. In 1941, when the Auditorium closed, the number of theaters had fallen to six with 28 productions, ten of which were musicals. The theaters did not begin to fill up again until after World War II.

As *Husbands Go* opened at the Blackstone on January 18, 1932, but as this flyer shows, moved to the Adelphi on February 14. It closed March 12, 1932. The Adelphi had a relatively short life. It opened in September 1923, and the last stage attraction closed December 3, 1932. It reopened as The Clark Theatre showing motion pictures.

THE STORY OF A
HUNGRY-HEARTED BANKER'S
WIFE FROM DUBUQUE WHO PICKED
UP A BOY FRIEND IN PARIS—

Charlie Lingard,
her husband, was rich
devoted and good enough—

AS HUSBANDS GO

BUT SHE WASN'T SATISFIED—

Champagne, gypsy music and suave lovemaking—

A hasty departure for Dubuque
to ask Charlie for a divorce—

Boy friend follows, is outsmarted when he goes into conference with Charlie over a bottle of Scotch and makes a fast trip back to the boulevards—

And now contentment reigns in the Lingard home, with a good sermon and a chicken dinner on Sunday, an evening at the movies and a few trips to Chicago each year to see the good shows.

HERE'S A PLAY THAT WILL
SET YOUR HEART AND YOUR
FUNNYBONE ATHROB!

RACHEL CROTHERS
wrote it and it's as smart and scintillating as "Let Us Be Gay"

JOHN GOLDEN
produced it and it's as gloriously human and humorous as "Lightnin'," "Seventh Heaven" or "That's Gratitude"

THE THEATRE GUILD
endorses it as one of the most glamorous performances of the past year on the New York stage and has offered it, with the complete New York cast, as the second production of the Guild subscription series in Chicago.

Moving Sunday Night, February 14

FROM THE BLACKSTONE THEATRE TO THE

ADELPHI CLARK AND MADISON 2 WEEKS ONLY

NIGHTS INCLUDING SUNDAY
POPULAR MATS. WEDNESDAY and SATURDAY

THE MAGAZINE
OF THE THEATRE

This beautiful cover was printed for *Three Little Girls*, which played at the Great Northern Theatre from September 21, 1930, until May 3, 1931. Occasionally programs would have listings of current attractions at other theaters and this one listed eight. One ad within the program booklet was for fine dining at Hotel Belmont for only $1.50!

The Goodman was built as a memorial for playwright Kenneth Sawyer Goodman in 1925. A repertory company played at the Goodman up until 1931, when the Goodman became the drama school within the Art Institute of Chicago. *The Golem*, the story of a mythological Jewish super hero, ran from May 7, 1929, through June 8th.

John T. McCutcheon, a newspaper cartoonist for the *Chicago Tribune*, also wrote a story that was serialized in that paper. Mary Aldis wrote a play based on this story, *An Heir at Large*, which was presented from December 17, 1925, through January 16, 1926, at the Goodman Theatre. The play was presented with cartoon settings and costumes, designed in black, white and gray by Mr. McCutcheon.

The Selwyn Theatre's interior was Georgian in character with walls of English walnut with very little carving. The whole effect was said to be one of simple richness, such as was found in the homes of the most discriminating. *Hollywood Holiday* played here from April 25th until June 8th in 1935.

The Selwyn and Harris Theaters were called the twin theaters when they opened in 1922. The exteriors may have been similar, but the interiors were very differently decorated though they had a similar elegance. The Harris was decorated with the Florentine flair of the 18th century with dark Italian walnut. This Stagebill is for *The Man Who Came to Dinner*, which ran from December 25, 1939 through June 1, 1940.

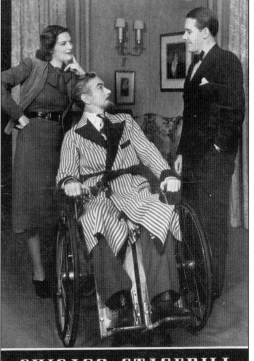

CHICAGO STAGEBILL

78

CHICAGO *Stagebill*

S. HUROK *presents*
Col. W. de BASIL'S
BALLET RUSSE
DE MONTE CARLO
AUDITORIUM THEATRE

PUBLISHED BY FIEBERG PRINTING CO., CHICAGO, ILL.

The Auditorium Theatre was built as a multifunctional building, housing the Theatre, offices, and a hotel. President Grover Cleveland laid the cornerstone of this Sullivan and Adler designed building in 1887, and President Benjamin Harrison dedicated the building in 1889. It was built to comfortably showcase singers and musicians as well as actors, statesmen, orators, and evangelists. Silent movies were also shown in the theater.

The building was renowned for having almost perfect acoustics, and the stage was 100-feet wide and 70-feet deep with 26 hydraulic lift sections to handle almost any production. The reducing curtain could be opened to 75 feet wide by 40 feet high or reduced to 47 feet wide and 35 feet high. The theater could be completely open with 4,200 seats or partially closed for smaller audiences.

Ballet Russe brought these ballets to Chicago in 1936. In 1939, there was a 50 year celebration for the Auditorium Theatre with a production of *Leave It To Me* starring Sophie Tucker. The theatre closed in 1941, and was used for a time as a servicemen's center.

Until October 1926, the Erlanger Theatre had been known as the Palace Music Hall. Later that month a new Palace Music Hall opened that featured vaudeville. This Playbill was for the new 1933 comedy, *When Ladies Meet*. Playing at the Princess was *Riddle Me This*. The Garrick had *On the Make*, Ethel Barrymore was at the Harris in *An Amazing Career*, and the Illinois featured *Shuffle Along*. These were all advertised in this Playbill.

Julius Caesar was the fare in 1938 at the Erlanger Theatre. This Chicago Stagebill had something new—"Who's Who in the Cast." Shakespeare was also being performed at the Grand Opera House, which placed ads in the Erlanger's program. *Room Service* was advertised at the Selwyn and *Father Malachy's Miracle* was advertised at the Harris.

Muriel Brassler and Tom Powers in "Julius Caesar"

The Blackfriars of the University of Chicago are one of the oldest university theater groups in the country. They were formally organized in 1904 though the group had been presenting entertainment since 1898. Pictured are the 1927 Blackfriars who wrote and presented *Plastered in Paris* that year. All parts were played by males since their charter excluded females from the stage.

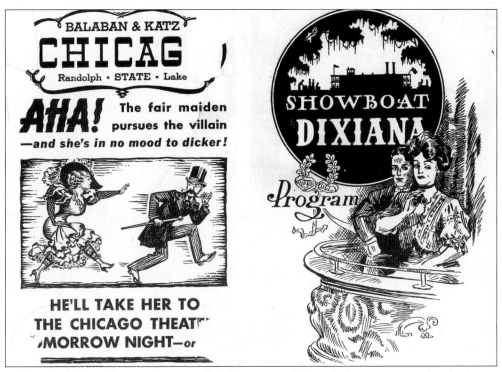

Balaban and Katz, of movie fame, produced a season of 10 melodramas presented in burlesque fashion on the showboat Dixiana, which was anchored in the north branch of the Chicago River at the Diversey Avenue bridge. The Colonial Bar on the second deck offered Budweiser beer for 10 cents a glass. For 30 cents you could get a chopped beefsteak with broiled Bermuda onions.

La Petit Gourmet restaurant at 619 N Michigan Avenue was one of the eateries that theatre patrons went to before or after the play for dinner. Restaurants were among the more popular advertisers in theater programs. When Clyde W. Riley was printing the programs, the Chicago cosmetic firm Djer-Kiss advertised on the front inside cover and Libby's canned peaches or catsup in the back inside cover.

Six

MOVIE PALACES

M otion pictures made their theatrical debut as part of a vaudeville shown in 1890. By 1912 Edison was producing reel-length talking pictures. Warner Brothers combined the phonograph with the motion picture using a special turntable that was synchronized to the projection motors. Then on October 6, 1927, *The Jazz Singer* with Al Jolson, a partial talkie, came out. Within a year, any picture of importance was produced as a talkie, and by 1930 silent films were a thing of the past. Color was first used in 1915 but it did not become commonplace until *Gone with the Wind* in 1939.

By 1907 there were 116 silent movie houses in Chicago, many of which were little more than storefronts with chairs, a screen, and a projector within, that catered to the lower class. The opening of Central Park Theater by Balaban and Katz in 1917 is regarded as the beginning of the movie palace era in Chicago. It seated 2,400 and had air conditioning! In the 1920s, movie houses became even larger and more elegant to draw the middle and upper class patrons in to view the full-length movies.

These new houses were designed by companies such as Rapp & Rapp in Chicago, John Everson, and Thomas Lamb to be over-the-top palaces, abundant in ornamentation. The decor was often in an Egyptian, Moorish, or Chinese style with plenty of marble, statues, fountains, paintings, and anything else that might enhance the "palace." Fancy decor gave movies a new respectability. The public loved these palaces! They lined up around the block, no matter what the picture, just to see and be seen in these palaces.

Barney Balaban's and Sam Katz's first venture into entertainment in 1908 was running a nickelodeon. After they added the Central Park Theater to their holdings, they began to be noticed in the business community. Ambitious young men, they continued building theaters using Rapp & Rapp as their architects for the extravaganzas such as the Tivoli, then the Chicago, Paradise, and the Uptown. At their peak, their chain had 125 theaters in the Midwest. In 1926, B & K merged with Paramount-Famous Players to form the Publix chain.

The Orpheum Theater was a typical early theater. It was built in 1907 as a vaudeville theater. In 1909, they added motion pictures and sing-a-longs. Slides such as the one for *Lend Me a Kiss Until To-morrow*, were used in theater sing-a-longs.

People such as Will Rogers played the circuit of theaters that included the Orpheum. Rogers was the star of Broadway and 71 movies of the 1920s and 1930s. His unsurpassed lariat feats, which he perfected in Wild West shows and then on vaudeville stages, were recorded in the classic movie, *The Ropin' Fool*.

The Randolph Theater, located at the northwest corner of State and Randolph Streets, opened in 1919 with 1,500 seats. It was a no-frills movie house without a stage and only an organ for music. Even though it was in the Loop, it was a second-run house that ran mostly westerns, war movies, and high-adventure pictures. When the palaces were built nearby, people who could not get seats in one might turn to the other for their entertainment. (Photo courtesy of Theater Historical Society of America, Elmhurst, Illinois.)

The first western movies were descendants of the Wild West Shows and dime novels. "They all have the same formula—two guns, bullets, 'pardner', a boy with a crooning voice, horses, and a sheriff. Its one big stew out of the same stewpot," so said "Broncho" Billy, the first movie cowboy. Early westerns were one-reelers consisting of little more than a chase and a fight.

Vendome Theater became one of Black Chicago's most popular movie theaters. Its popular house orchestra was led by Erskine Tate. When Louis Armstrong moved to the Vendome after performing at Dreamland Café, the crowds went wild! Other jazz artists who performed at the Vendome during the 1920s included pianist Earl Hines, drummer Jimmy Bertrand, cornetist Freddie Keppard, and pianist Lil Hardin-Armstrong.

The Biograph Theater is one of Chicago's oldest remaining neighborhood movie houses. It's construction is typical of those first-generation movie houses. Inside this simple building is a storefront-width lobby, a recessed entrance, and a free standing ticket booth. The Biograph was designed by Samuel N. Crowen with 1,000 seats in 1914. Today, it is best known as the place outside of which public enemy number one, John Dillinger, died in 1934.

This photograph of Randolph Street looking west from State Street shows a lively theater district with both movies and live stage shows. Movies typically would be shown in loop for six to eight weeks, then move to outlying theaters in the city and suburbs. The younger generation of the middle and well-to-do classes were the major patrons of these movie palaces. They came to escape the cares of the day and see how the wealthy lived, dressed, and misbehaved in films by such legendary directors as Cecil B. DeMille. Movie companies like Warner Brothers and M-G-M produced hundreds of films a year, many of them musicals.

Motion pictures were not the only thing these patrons came to see in these palaces. There were elaborate stage shows in the B & K theaters and any theater of any reputation had live music, usually an organ and an ensemble of players. Some playbills even featured the organist or orchestra over the feature film.

This magnificent Art Deco theater lobby set piece for permanent display was made for a Chicago theater by artist Charles Stanis in 1934. The piece is finished in blue, white, and silver. The display panel is covered with velour for appliqué work.

Movie palaces vied with one another to create indoor and outdoor displays that were flashy, full of motion and lots of lights. Lobby displays such as this one were created by designers who used glass, tubing, wall board, paper, cut-outs, motion devices, chromium letters, oil cloth, shadow boxes, lamps, lumber, and foil paper to work their magic.

88

The balcony area of the Chicago Theatre was designed by Rapp & Rapp to remind one of a seventeenth century French palace. It had a five-story grand lobby and a three-story interior lobby. Imagine listening to a pianist who was seated here in that grand space. The organ in the main theater was played by Jesse Crawford. Helen Anderson Crawford joined him at a second console after their marriage.

NEXT SUNDAY NOON
Chicago Theatre Sunday Noon Musical Hour
MISS BASEL CRISTOL
Solo Organist
and the
CHICAGO THEATRE CONCERT ENSEMBLE

SUNDAY, MAY 2, 1926
11:45 A. M. to 12:45

1.	Prelude	Rachmaninoff
	MISS CRISTOL	

The next four by
THE CHICAGO THEATRE CONCERT ENSEMBLE

2.	Selections from "Werther"	Massenet
3.	Mignonette	Friml
4.	Traume	Wagner
5.	Wine, Woman and Song	Strauss
6.	Soloist	

The next four by
THE CHICAGO THEATRE CONCERT ENSEMBLE

7.	Overture to "Romeo and Juliet"	Tschaikowsky
8.	La Cinquantaine	Gabriel-Marie
9.	Scarf Dance	Chaminade
10.	March Militaire	Schubert
11.	Morning, Noon and Night	Suppe
	MISS CRISTOL	

Doors Open at 10:20 A.M. with feature picture

COLLEEN MOORE
IN
"IRENE"

BALABAN & KATZ
CHICAGO THEATRE
"The Wonder Theatre of the World"

Lake State Street *Randolph*

Chicago Theatre Sunday Noon Musical Hour

HENRI A. KEATES, Organist,
THELMA BOLLINGER, Contralto
and
THE CHICAGO THEATRE
CONCERT ENSEMBLE

SUNDAY, APRIL 25, 1926
At Eleven Forty-five o'Clock

The movie wasn't the only attraction of going to the Chicago Theatre. The awesome architecture was certainly a draw. The Chicago also hosted many vaudeville acts, dance troupes, beauty pageants, and classical and jazz concerts. If you look hard at this program, you will find the name of the movie, but you can't miss what the live entertainment was.

The Chicago Theatre opened on October 26, 1921 with the film *The Sign on the Door* starring Norma Talmadge. She was considered one of the most chic of the silent screen stars, but she was one of those who did not make the transition to talkies. A capacity crowd filled the theater on opening night. By the end of the 1920s, with the rise of "talkies," many theater organs went "silent."

The Oriental Theater, like the Chicago, had a Mighty Wurlitzer. In keeping with the gimmicked world of "Arabian Nights" in which the theater was designed by Rapp & Rapp, the organ is ornate, even with crimson fire birds on the sides. What a sight that must have been rising from the floor!

The Oriental Theater opened with a flourish on May 8, 1926. It was said that the theater was designed as a showcase for Paul Ash and his Merry-Mad Musical Gang. Elaborate stage shows were created by Frank Cambria for Balaban and Katz in the 1920s and *Insultin' the Sultan* was one of these. Have you found the name of the movie in the ad yet? It's there, but small.

The interior of the Oriental Theater was designed by Rapp & Rapp as a world of Scheherezade and magic carpets. A press release suggested that "To study and examine the array of sculptured detail throughout the theatre is like a trip to the Orient. The auditorium is beyond description with its intricacies of Eastern magnificence, grotesque dancers, and Indian animal figures, resplendent with lights behind colored glass around ornate shrine-like niches." So it was.

The Marbro Theater was built by Louis and Meyer Marks to serve the West Side. They named it after themselves, Mar(ks) bro(thers). The Marbro, which opened May 28, 1927, was one of the largest movie theaters outside the Loop with 5,200 seats. This ad stresses the movie, unlike earlier Balaban and Katz ads, over the other attractions, unusual for the 1920s when patrons expected more for their money than just a movie.

The Marbro was designed by Levy and Klein with a Wurlitzer organ (this one with five ranks) and a spectacular lobby with a grand staircase and crystal chandelier. This later picture shows the exterior with the large sign taking the eye away from the ornate building. The Marks brothers had a chain of local theaters, but they retired from the entertainment business in 1928. (Photo by J. Johnson Jr., CHI 34982, courtesy of Chicago Historical Society.)

The interior of the Avalon was designed by John Eberson. His interiors were less ornate than the Rapp & Rapp interiors. His trademark was twinkling stars and cloud formation on the theater's ceiling. The Avalon was designed to remind the patron of a Turkish palace. The minarets housed some of the organ pipes and a fountain is in the niche between them.

Movie palaces needed a great many workers. There were up to 30 ushers in many of them, all in uniform and drilled to be precise in their work. It was a desirable job for a young man. In other areas of the country, girls could also be ushers, but in Chicago it was a boy's job. There were also uniformed maids in the ladies rooms and footmen in the lobby.

The Music Box, a neighborhood theater with 750 seats featuring second-run films, opened August 22, 1929. The Theater was designed with an orchestra pit and organ chambers—just in case "talkies" didn't take off. There was no stage so it was destined be a movie house in any case.

When gold bonds were offered for sale to build this complex in 1925, a 25-year lease had already been signed with Balaban & Katz for a motion picture house in the building. This was to become the Norshore on Howard Street. It opened the next year. This theatre was to have no balconies or galleries, according to the bond ad.

Seven

OF THEE I SING

Chicago was the "Second City" of sheet music publishing at the end of the 19th century and the first decades of the 20th. Sheet music of the latest vaudeville hits and musicals from stage and screen was quickly published by dozens of publishers in Chicago. The subjects chosen to sing about and the sentiments of the songs act as a chronicle of attitudes in each decade. Older songs up through World War I were sentimental, romantic, or patriotic in nature. After the war, songs dealt with having fun with a great deal more sexuality in their lyrics. Older sheet music was often very racist against Blacks, Germans, Irish, Jews, and Native Americans, while later sheet music poked fun at other new immigrants. Sheet music, which could be purchased for 25 cents during most of these decades, made its way into thousands of homes in Chicago. Young piano players, tired of playing serious music, rebelled and were eager customers for the latest rag, fox trot, or Charleston.

Some of the images found on sheet music, offensive as they might be to modern readers, were never the less vivid examples of how people saw Chicago's arriving cultures. This reaction to a changing ethnic landscape was not unique to Chicago, but one shared by people in most cities in the United States. Once these immigrant groups became entrenched in the big cities, music publishers reversed gears and published songs of a positive nature to increase sales.

Songs about Chicago were popular sellers, but one alone, *Chicago, That Tottlin' Town,* has remained fixed in the public mind.

I Miss Thee was published in 1898 by Lyon and Healy in Chicago. Shown here is the central portion of the music's romantic music cover. The song was written by Lydia Olive Green.

"I Miss Thee, I Miss Thee So, The Killdee bird flies from the nest...
All the while as wild flow'rs grow, I Miss Thee So."

Musical Supplement to the SUNDAY CHRONICLE
Chicago, Sunday, Mar. 17th 1901.

GATH'RING THE SHAMROCKS WITH PATSIE

Dedicated by the AUTHOR
to
CALLIE MULVANEY

Words and Music
by
HARRY P. KEILY.

By 1901 the Irish in Chicago were firmly established in the economic and political life of the city. The old days of hatred for the thousands of newly arrived Irish, who were eager for jobs and willing to displace workers by working for less, were over. The March 17, 1901, *Gath'ring The Shamrocks with Patsie*, by Harry P. Keily, surely increased newspaper sales in the Irish community. The lyrics drip with nostalgia for Ireland.

> *"Every night and day I ever pray*
> *For those we left behind", and*
> *"I wish that I could wander*
> *In those fragrant meadow green*
> *And Greet my love,*
> *Who vowed I was his darling Irish Queen."*

The second Annual Pageant of Progress in Chicago in 1922 had a new song called *Push Along, Chicago!* with music and lyrics by Wirt Denison.

"Where lake and sky are meeting,
In comprehensive greeting,
There's a city fair as jewels in a crown.
The people there are snappy,
Their lives are hale and happy.
"Chicago" is the name of this great town.
The parks abound in pleasure. The theatres
give full measure,
The railroads give fine service ev'ry
where;
The boulevards are spacious…"

Between the two World's Fairs in Chicago there was a series of festivals held in the 1920s called Pageants of Progress. In 1921, the *Chicago Herald Examiner* sponsored a song writing contest for that year's pageant with a prize of $2,000 going to the winning songwriter. *Hail, Chicago!* with words by Ted Turnquist and music by Bob Allen was a short, hymn-like tune that was easy to sing and easy to forget in only a few days. More popular songs about Chicago were *Chicago Rhythm*, *Chicago Blues*, *I'm From Chicago*, and *Chicago Stomp*.

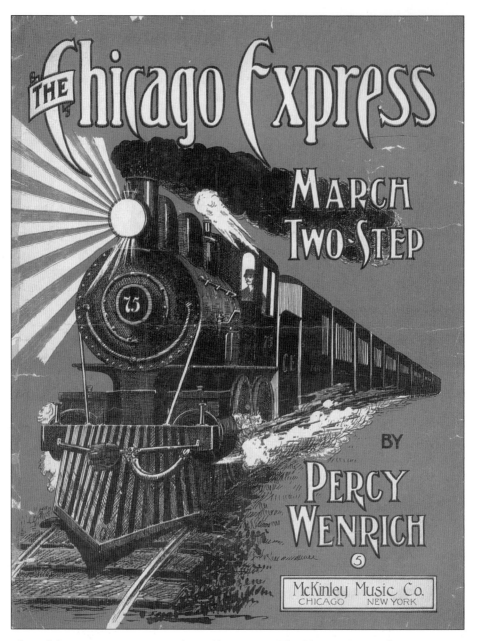

Another of the many songs written about Chicago was *The Chicago Express* that was a two-step march by popular Chicago pianist and composer Percy Wenrich. It was published by McKinley Music Co. and featured a racing locomotive on the cover. Wenrich, a white musician who played hot piano was called "The Joplin Kid." He recorded piano rolls in the studio of Imperial Roll Company in Chicago.

Wenrich, born in Missouri, started his musical career in vaudeville then later became a song writer in Tin Pan Alley. He was an accomplished pianist, but made his money writing sentimental old fashioned songs. His songs *When You Wore a Tulip and I Wore a Red, Red Rose* and *Put on Your Old Gray Bonnet* were first thought to be too corny and homey by his publishers. But when the sheet music hit Chicago streets, they sold like hot cakes!

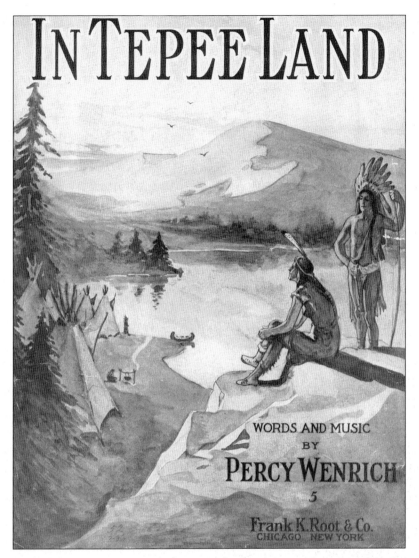

IN TEPEE LAND

WORDS AND MUSIC
BY
PERCY WENRICH

5

Frank K. Root & Co.
CHICAGO   NEW YORK

Percy Wenrich also cashed in, along with countless other music writers, on the profitable theme of Indian Romeos and Juliets. Chicago's Frank K. Root & Co. published his popular song called *In Tepee Land*, which transferred white culture versions of romance and love onto Native Americans.

*"Big Chief went a wooing, just like a dove a
cooing,
His dream of love pursuing a pale faced maid
promising a
Heap wedding day, if you'll only come and live
in my Tepee."
Great Big Indian Chief, Loved little pale faced
maid;
It was his belief of him she was afraid.
So he went a wooing, just like a dove a cooing,
His dream of life pursuing away; Then one night*

*moon was bright,
To the maid he did say,*

Chorus:

*Oh! won't you come with me and live in my
Tepee,
There we will happy be, no one but you and me,
Round camp fires burning bright, Our hearts will
e'er be light,
The Indians say Heap wedding day."*

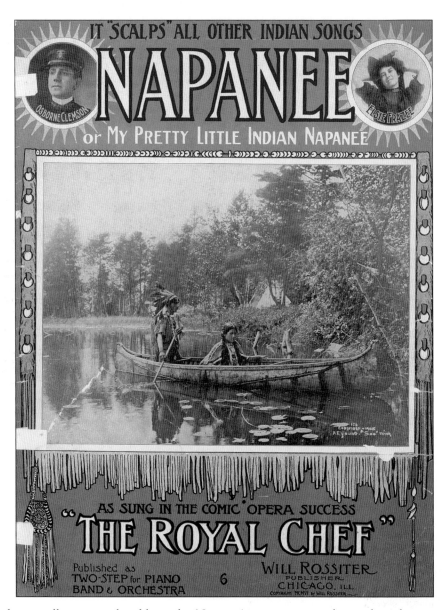

Another excellent example of how the Native Americans were depicted in sheet music is *Napanee* or *My Pretty Little Indian Napanee*. Emblazoned on the cover is the caption "It Scalps All Other Indian Songs." The song was arranged as a two-step from a comic opera called *The Royal Chief* and was published by Will Rossiter of Chicago. It was supposed to be based on a "true story" about "Big Chief Spare the Rod's" daughter falling in love with a white con-man willing, according to the lyrics:

> "Sun burn to a darker shade, I'll wear feathers on my head,
> Paint my face an Indian Red" if she would marry him.
> Sorry to say, his 'con' talk caught her, soon he married the Big Chief's daughter,
> "Happiest couple that you ever say, Till his dream of love had faded,
> Napanee looked old and jaded, Just about like any other Squaw...
> Soon papooses came in numbers, Redskin yeils disturbed his slumbers."

Good Bye Mary Dear, published by Frank K. Root & Co. with music by Percy Wenrich, was a typical song of the day that described a romance broken by war. It is a tear-jerker; the young man does not return.

> *"He bravely fought and fell, In the thickest of the fray...*
> *He whispered soft and low, As his young life ebbed away,*
> *Good Bye Mary Dear."*

It was common practice to take famous melodies from the classics and put them into another rhythmic pattern. All the swing bands did it, and so did earlier composers. George L. Cobb interpolated Rachmaninoff's famous *Prelude* and called the work *Russian Rag*. The song was included in a musical of the day and Mlle. Rea danced to it. Publisher Will Rositer was located at 71 West Randolph Street.

Axel Christensen wrote and published one of the most delicious rags ever, called *The Cauldron Rag* in 1909. Christensen called himself a publisher of popular music, and certainly during this time, rag-time was popular. Ragtime, later jazz, and boogie woogie were often called the "Devil's Music." Many a preacher cautioned his flock against such music and against those who wrote it or danced to it.

Sheet music publishers rarely credited the artist who designed the cover art. Just as with other forms of selling goods, a good illustration went a long way towards selling what was inside. McKinley Music Company's *Chanticleer (Cock-a-doodle-doo)* by Richard Grant is an excellent example of effective commercial art. The rooster is a flaming red with yellow legs. The title was printed in black with a light blue background.

Sheet music covers, like this cover, for ragtime tunes were bold and eye catching. Some of the most popular rags of the day, such as *Maple Leaf Rag*, were written by Scott Joplin. *Chanticleer* was billed as a Rag-March-Waltz. Musicologists define jazz as part rag, part march, and part blues—making this piece of music by Richard Grand more of a jazz composition than pure ragtime. Although Irving Berlin wrote a popular song called *Alexander's Rag Time Band*, the song, ironically, was not really a rag but a catchy fox trot!

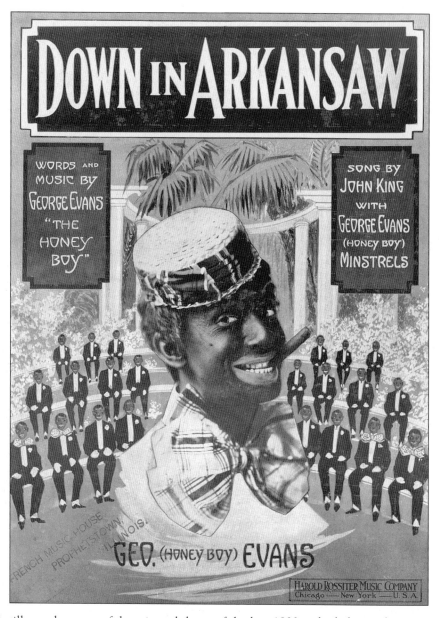

Vaudeville was born out of the minstrel shows of the late 1800s, which featured various acts of interest for the whole family. These early minstrel shows were performed by black artists, but when the shows became popular, white booking agents expanded the number of performing groups by offering white minstrel shows that were "black face," meaning white performers who were enacting the parts of real black musicians.

Will Rossiter published *Down in Arkansaw*. The song and lyrics were written by George Evens, "The Honey Boy," who was the star of his own minstrel company. The lyrics show the demeaning humor of the day.

"Had a Girl, her name was Til,…
Liver lips and face so black,
Was so cross-eyed for a fac."

W.J. Cunningham created a cover for the sheet music for *Ma Ca'Line* that surely made copies fly out the music store door. Against a red background with dramatic use of yellow for the tires, male driver's jacket, hat of the female, and song title, he created this artistic cover. It is marred by the racist depiction of the two riders, yet was very sellable in a time when African-Americans were shamelessly made fun of by the white population. Lyon and Healy, a famous Chicago music store, published the song, which is a rag, as "A Zulu Spasm in Three Fits." Although the cover of this piece of sheet music states that the words and music were by Ben Tuttle, and arrangement was by J.E. Hartel, there were no printed lyrics on the music. One can only imaging how racist the words probably were.

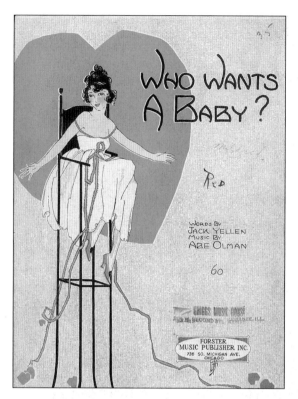

Who Wants A Baby? as a modern title for a song might be misconstrued, but back in 1929 it meant who wants a babe, the lingo of the day. With words by Jack Yellen and music by Abe Olman, this was a typical fun-loving romp published by Forster on Michigan Avenue. A few lyrics tell all about the song,

> "You know that every baby,
> Should have a daddy dear."

Forster Music Publisher, Inc., located on South Wabash, noted that their sheet music was compatible with the arrangement heard on the radio and found on piano rolls. Axel Christensen's 1923 hit *Nobody's Business* was a typical early-1920s song but unique in that it had no lyrics. Instead it was a fast-paced novelty number. The cover illustration by Van Dorn Morgan equates chattering girls with the general sound of the song.

106

One of the 19th century's hottest mammas who wailed her bluesy-like songs of love was Sophie Tucker. Forster issued the sheet music of a song with a tongue-in-cheek reference to Tucker teaching little children called *Learning*. The lyrics are typical Tucker, who helped write the song.

> "I always thought that I knew a lot,
> But what I forgot, would fill a book, or two;
> For since I met a certain girl, My poor brain is in a whirl,
> And that girl is you: I find I'm Learning something new,
> Each day since I have been with you;
> You taught me readin', writin', and some spellin',
> I'm not tellin', other things your teaching brings,
> I'm learning pretty words—and certain things I've never heard,
> So, I'm confessin' You taught me my lesson, It's 'I Love You.'"

107

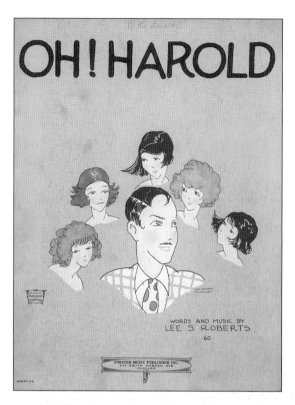

In 1929, Forster published *Oh! Harold* with words and music by Lee S. Roberts. Roberts wrote hundreds of songs and recorded hundreds of piano rolls.

"Oh! Gracious, I'm just a bit audacious,
My pulse is weak, I need a Sheik."

There were many songs published in Chicago that began with "Oh!". In 1917, Forster issued the famous song *Oh Johnny, Oh Johnny, Oh!* with music by Abe Olman and words by Ed Rose.

If ever a song was historically prophetic, it was the 1930 tune *I Feel Pessimistic* from the Broadway smash hit, *Good News*, that was later made into a movie by Metro-Goldwyn-Mayer. This song captures the essence of the care-free 1920s but adds a dose of impending disaster with the lyrics,

"We went out spendin' my dough,
Kept right on even when she said no"

The movie was one of the top box office hits in Chicago that year.

A suggestive song of the day in 1926 was *In June When the Moon Loves to Spoon* published by Charlotte Goll Music Publishing Company in Chicago. The young couple on the cover is doing their own spooning. The moon played a prominent role in the lyrics of many songs.

> *"Don't seem to have any trouble, Don't even feel the rain,*
> *Life floats along like a bubble, the reason, let me explain.*
> *In June, when the moon loves to spoon with the stars,*
> *and Mars is waiting his turn,   then you and I,*
> *We'll say goodbye, and let the old world churn,*
> *Like a star from afar, we'll forget who we are,*
> *We'll remember spent cares no more. In a sweet little nest,*
> *You know the rest..."*

Rudy Vallee was one of the superstars of the 1920s in his roles as actor, singer, saxophone player, and big band leader. He used a megaphone to croon to his audiences. *I'm Still Caring*, written by Vallee and John Klenner, was published by Forster Music Publisher of Chicago in 1929. Typical Valle lyrics are,

> *"I'm still caring, I'm still sharing*
> *The golden dreams that you and I once knew."*

Forster Music Publisher also published three song books by Art Shefte which instructed young piano players in the new music of the day. Their *Jazz Breaks* had 150 new and original breaks full of "the tricks, the clever breaks, the snappy endings." The *Hot Breaks* defined hot as "jingly, jumpy, jerky. Music with a kick full of force and fire." "Sort of a wail. Not exactly melancholy, but plaintive, drawling and pleading, almost crying," was how the book *Blue Breaks* described the blues. If this description is accurate of the blues, then Rudy Vallee's wailing was certainly a form of the blues!

Eight
RADIO DAYS

When we talk of entertainment in Chicago, radio and television come immediately to mind. But before 1920, there was neither of these in town. The first broadcast from a radio crystal set was from Pittsburgh with the election returns of the Harding-Cox presidential race. Individuals, businesses, and institutions were quick to see the potential that radio held and acquired federal licenses to establish their own stations all across the country. By 1923 Chicago had three stations, but White's Log Book shows 24 Chicago stations by 1928! In 1929, there were nine firms engaged in the production of radios in Chicago, and in 1931 the city's yellow pages showed 123 manufacturers of radios or radio parts.

Radio programming was simple in the beginning. Music, especially classical, was played and announcers read the news or sport scores. Lectures on domestic topics were popular. There were no commercials, no sound effects, and most performers were unpaid. Soon networks of stations were created and NBC's red and blue networks were the first in 1926. CBS was founded in 1927.

Chicago radio blossomed in the 1930s with the creation of dramatic programs, detective programs, comedies, soap operas, amateur entertainment, and broadcast journalism. Musical programs that were broadcast from local ballrooms and jazz clubs gained in popularity. Swing music was made popular through the radio from coast to coast, not only in big cities but also in rural America.

Amos 'n' Andy, created in Chicago, became a national hit. Chicago was known for the many soap operas that were written and produced by Chicago stations. And who can forget the WLS *National Barn Dance*, which aired every Saturday night or *Jack Armstrong, the All American Boy* that came on the air five days each week!

And what of television? The first broadcast in Chicago was in 1929 with Milton Berle performing on a closed-circuit telecast. There were many experimental television stations in the 1930s with W9XAP being among the first to transmit from Chicago in 1930.

Do you remember hearing, "It's a beautiful day in Chicago," from WMAQ radio each day?

This map shows where you might have been when you heard it. During a one year period, letters were received from people reporting reception of WMAQ in the areas shown here. WMAQ was owned by *The Chicago Daily News*.

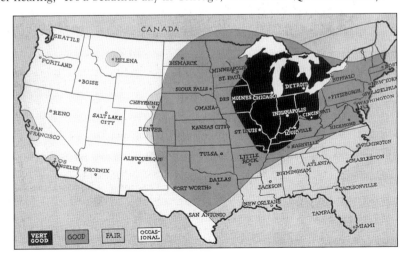

Newspapers and individuals published guides to radio stations all over the United States and Canada. These early directories gave space to record where the listener found that station. This 1939 White's Radio Log was published bimonthly in New York. The owner of this copy kept a list of where on the dial he found the stations.

This ad for WMAQ's new broadcasting station was printed in the official program for the Seventh Annual Chicago Radio Show held at the Coliseum on October 8-14, 1928. Demonstrations of television were held several times each day, and various Chicago radio stations WMAQ, KYW, WLS, WENR, WGES, WGN, WHT, and WSBC broadcast samples of their regular or special programs through the afternoons and evenings.

Opposite: Chicago-based Sears, Roebuck and Co. began offering radios in its 1919 fall catalog as a novelty item. This radio had to be hand assembled by its owner. Radios were first advertised as a "perfect gift" during the 1922 Christmas season. By 1925 radio stations dotted the map all across the country and had developed stronger signal patterns. Sears offered a Silvertone Neutrodyne radio set with speaker on the top for $88.75.

Most radio sets were run by batteries at first or something other than alternating current, the standard in American homes. Rival Montgomery Ward sold six radio sets priced from $31.74 for a small mantel radio to $56.95 for its most expensive set, a console battery driven set. Here is their $39.85, 7 Tube Airline, All Electric Super Heterodyne radio. For only five dollars down, you too could join the technological revolution. By 1931 there were almost 16 million radio sets in the United States. Many were in rural areas that had not been electrified. Those sets were still run with batteries.

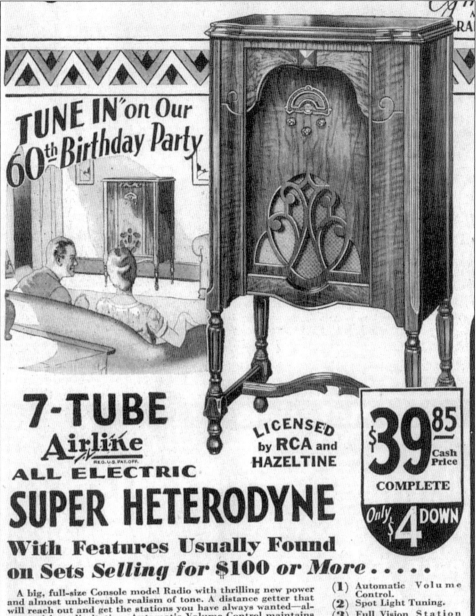
113

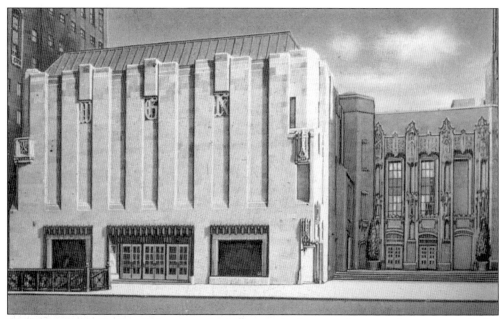

The *Chicago Tribune* supplied news and market reports for several stations beginning with the first Chicago station, KYW, until 1924 when WGN, Inc. was formed as a Tribune subsidiary. One of the early features was the reading of *Chicago Tribune* comics on Sundays. WGN studios are linked to the Tribune Tower on North Michigan Avenue.

Early studios used draperies everywhere for sound control. At first, radio stations used pianos but later organs were also used for a richer sound. Today, WGN has one of the few old studio organs left in the United States, but it has been moved to its television studios. It was used to accompany programs such as *Little Orphan Annie* and a program called *Pipe Dreams*. (Photo courtesy of WGN.)

Pat Barnes was the Director-Announcer of station WHT in the early 1920s. One of his programs featured reading poetry on the air. *Pat Barnes Pickups*, printed in 1927, is a collection of the poems that he read on the air and was dedicated "To you, dear friend, of the unseen audience."

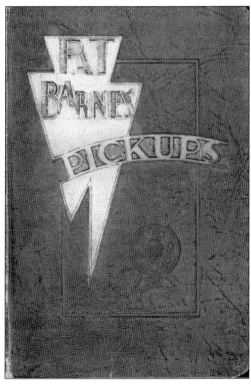

Pick-ups

We pick up a thought,
And it lasts all the day,
We pick up a work
That cheers on our way.

We pick up a friend
Who holds through the years.
We pick up, if we will,
More of joy, than of tears.

We pick up the book,
And we pick up a smile;
'Tis these happy pick-ups
That make life worth the while.

—P.B.

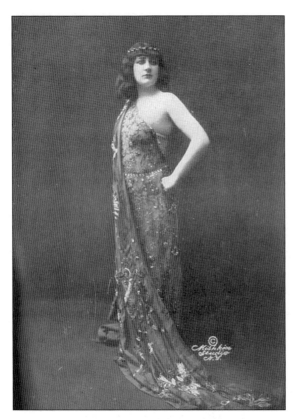

Station KYW was founded in 1921 specifically to broadcast opera in Chicago. In 1922, Mary Garden, who had been with the Chicago Grand Opera Company since 1910, was asked to be its director for one year. She was said to have caused more excitement on the Chicago opera scene, off stage and on, than any other singer in the company's history. She continued singing with the company until 1930.

WGN broadcast concerts by the Chicago Symphony Orchestra beginning with those during the 1933-1934 Century of Progress. Some of the concerts broadcast were from the Grant Park band stand, pictured above.

Joseph and Pasquale Gallicchio were both connected with station WMAQ in 1931. Joseph (right) was the musical director for the station with previous experience as violinist with the Chicago Civic Opera. Joseph joined WMAQ in 1927 and built an orchestra of 21 members to provide music for the station. His brother, Pasquale (left), was the announcer with WMAQ who opened the station at six each morning.

Radio programming has changed a great deal since the early 1920s when stations ran schedules such as the one shown on this WENR program schedule. The times between those listed probably were filled with recorded music, news, or stock and sports announcements.

W-E-N-R
PROGRAM SCHEDULE
(Effective until further notice)
344.5 meters—870 kilocycles

WEEKDAYS
10:00 am. to 10:30 am.—Sunshine Hour
11:15 am. to 11:45 am.—Home Service Hour
5:00 pm. to 5:30 pm.—Children's Hour
7:15 pm. to 7:30 pm.—Farmer Rusk

WEEKNIGHTS
(Variety Programs)
11:00 pm. to 2:00 am.—Monday
9:00 pm. to 2:00 am.—Tuesday
9:00 pm. to 2:00 am.—Wednesday
11:00 pm. to 2:00 am.—Thursday
11:30 pm. to 2:00 am.—Friday
12:00 midnight
to 2:00 am.—Saturday

SUNDAY
10:00 am. to 11:00 am.—Sunshine Hour
11:00 am. to 12:15 pm.—Central Church
2:30 pm. to 6:00 pm.—Popular Program
8:00 pm. to 9:30 pm.—Downers Grove Sunday Evening Club
9:30 pm. to 11:00 pm.—Edison Symphony Orchestra
11:00 pm. to 2:00 am.—Variety Program

MIKE AND HERMAN
4:00 pm.—Sunday
11:30 pm.—Monday, Tuesday, Wednesday, Thursday, Friday

ADAM AND EVA
Midnight daily, except Saturday

Some churches considered radio to be like much of the music of the day, too worldly and distracting. Other religious leaders felt that the radio could be used to expand their missionary work. The Bergstroms, Lois and Reuben, who constituted one half of the Little Brown Church Quartet, broadcast in WLS in the 1930s each Sunday afternoon.

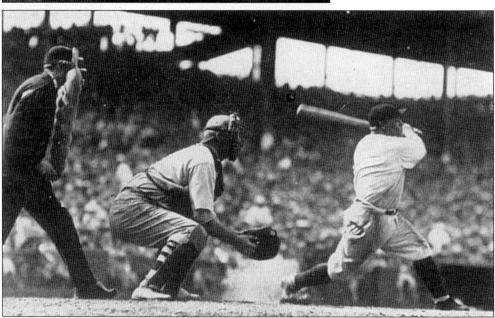

Sports announcing was an early part of radio. Blow-by-blow descriptions of boxing matches were broadcast as early as July of 1921, a running description of the 1921 World Series was aired, and football was on the air waves on a regular basis by 1922. WMAQ broadcast major league baseball games each day directly from the ball park beginning in 1925 with Hal Totten as announcer.

Freidman Gosden and Charles Carrell developed two black characters, Sam and Henry, in the minstrel style based on a cartoon strip in the 1920s. The tales of Sam and Henry that they wrote and performed on WGN became favorites in Chicago. They were on WGN as Sam 'n' Henry for five years before moving to WMAQ in 1928.

Sam 'n' Henry changed their names to Amos 'n' Andy on WMAQ and their antics were told and retold all over the nation. From March 1930 to February 1931, 37 percent of all radio owners listened to the program. Motion picture houses and department stores would stop and tune in to the broadcasts so their patrons would not miss an episode.

Burridge D. Butler   Hal O'Halloran   "Arkie"   Carl Davis   John Lair   "Slim" Miller   Linda Parker   Lul

Glenn Snyder   Max Terhune   Eddie Allen   Mac and Bob   The Three Little Maids   Red

Red Foley   "Harty" Taylor   The Hoosier Sod-Busters   C. V. Gregory

Edit. Prairie Farmer   "Spareribs"   "Uncle Ezra"   "Hiram"   Fleming Allen   Bill Vickland   John O'Connor   Harry Steele   Program Director

John Brown   Rube Tronson   L. Brusoe   Grace Wilson   George Biggar

WLS (World's Largest Store) was named by Sears Roebuck and Company, who first owned the station. This puzzle featured the cast of the weekly WLS *Barn Dance*, sometime in the early 1930s. The program was broadcast from a stage in the Eighth Street Theatre. Perhaps you recognize Red Foley on the top, ninth from the left, or George Goebel, seventh down on the left. WLS was the Prairie Farmer Station. The *Prairie Farmer* magazine and WLS were used to serve farmers in Illinois and Indiana with a balance of farm programs and wholesome entertainment for farm families. The 1934 WLS Family Album was dedicated "To all of you who have faith, who believe in the things that are beautiful, good and true, who hold sacred the family fireside, and who seek the happiness that comes from kindly service."

These fellows broadcast a "barn dance" from an airplane flying over Chicago. On the far right is Hal O'Halloran who, according to studio tradition, would sing *Asleep in the Deep* to fill in if anything broke down during a program. In the early days of radio, he must have sung often.

Little Orphan Annie was played on the radio by Shirley Bell, shown here with her arm around Allan Baruck, who is seated. This immensely popular program began in 1930 and sold a lot of Ovaltine. Do you remember, "Who's that little chatterbox? The one with the pretty auburn locks? Who can it be? It's Little Orphan Annie." Kids went wild over the *Lone Ranger, Captain Midnight, Tom Mix and his Straight Shooters, Little Orphan Annie,* and *Jack Armstrong:* all Chicago programs. These were aired after school and before bedtime on week nights. (Photo courtesy of WGN.)

Daytime soap operas were big in the 1930s and many of them were produced by Chicago radio stations. Actors often played more than one part in these serialized stories. Housewives got so involved in the problems of characters in *Guiding Light*, *The Woman in White*, or *Ma Perkins* that they were able to temporarily forget their own problems. After dinner, families often got together to listen to their favorite shows. (Photo courtesy of WGN.)

Networks had large house bands or orchestras, and every major studio had a telephone line to various night spots. The Benny Goodman Band was playing at the Congress Hotel for a six-month period in 1935 at a time when big band broadcasts were heard coast to coast. The dance music called swing was largely popularized through radio.

GOOD
MORNING
BREAKFAST
CLUBBER

GOOD
MORNIN'
TO YA!

Don McNeill's Breakfast Club was a variety show with pleasant morning banter, gentle humor, and music. Produced and aired from Chicago, it was one of the shows that stayed here when others were moving to the coasts. Fran Allison, later of *Kukla, Fran & Ollie,* played Aunt Fanny, who gave home-spun gossip and advice. Anita Bryant and Johnny Desmond played on the Breakfast Club before going on in their careers.

On September 14, 1934, the first broadcast of the *Morris B. Sachs Amateur Hour* originated in a show window of the Morris B. Sachs store at 6638 South Halsted Street. The show had to be moved to an auditorium near the store within a few weeks because the crowds were stopping traffic! The sponsor of the popular show, of course, was Morris B. Sachs Clothing Store.

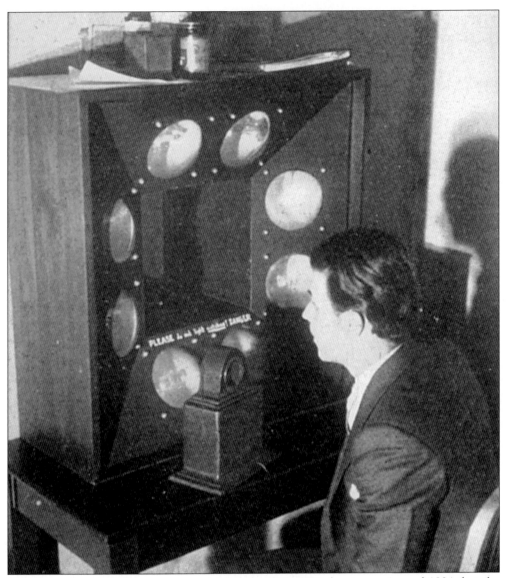

The theory for television was patented in Germany in 1884, but it wasn't until 1924 that the first demonstration of television was made. Standards were still not set as to the number of lines, or definition, and the number of frames per second that would be shown when experimental television was authorized to be broadcast in several cities by the Federal Radio Commission. By 1931 television station W9XAP in Chicago had been licensed to *The Daily News*. The station aired daily except on Sundays.

The new television station worked with WMAQ to show "playlets" with the pictures of the costumed characters being shown on W9XAP and the sound heard on WMAQ. As many as five figures at a time could be broadcast with equipment that included the microvisor shown above. Other programming features included singers and dancers, boxing and wrestling matches, and people reading aloud. Visitors were welcome to visit the reception room and watch the television when shows were being broadcast.

Regular television broadcasting did not begin until 1941 in the United States, and many industry standards were not completely set until the 1950s.

Index